BOUND TOGETHER

Baptism, Eucharist, and the Church

SHAWN O. STROUT

Copyright © 2024 Shawn Strout

All rights reserved. No part of this book may be reproduced, stored in a retrieval system, or transmitted in any form or by any means, electronic or mechanical, including photocopying, recording, or otherwise, without the written permission of the publisher.

Unless otherwise noted, the Scripture quotations are from New Revised Standard Version Bible, copyright © 1989 National Council of the Churches of Christ in the United States of America. Used by permission. All rights reserved worldwide.

Seabury Books
19 East 34th Street
New York, NY 10016
www.churchpublishing.org

Seabury Books is an imprint of Church Publishing Incorporated

Cover design by Newgen
Typeset by Nord Compo

ISBN 978-1-64065-732-8 (paperback)
ISBN 978-1-64065-733-5 (eBook)

Library of Congress Control Number: 2024938951

As many of you as were baptized into Christ have clothed yourselves with Christ (Gal 3:27).

The cup of blessing that we bless, is it not a sharing in the blood of Christ?
The bread that we break, is it not a sharing in the body of Christ?
Because there is one bread, we who are many are one body,
for we all partake of the one bread (1 Cor 10:16-17).

CONTENTS

Acknowledgments vii
Abbreviations ix
Introduction xi

1. Jesus' Table Fellowship, Baptism, and the Eucharist 1

2. Baptism, the Eucharist, and the History of the Church 29
   An Indissoluble Bond

3. Baptism, the Eucharist, and the Liturgy of the Church 75
   A Baptismal-Eucharistic Liturgical Theology

4. Baptism and the Eucharist Make the Church 109
   A Baptismal-Eucharistic Ecclesiology

5. Baptism and the Eucharist Connect the Church 151
   Ecumenical Perspectives

Conclusion 181
Bibliography 187
Index 199

ACKNOWLEDGMENTS

This book began over a decade ago. I am deeply indebted to the late Rt. Rev. Mark Dyer, D.D. and the Rev. Gordon Lathrop, Ph.D., who provided necessary nuance to its earlier form and valuable support for a budding scholar. I continue to be grateful to the Rev. Ian S. Markham, Ph.D., and the Rev. Melody Knowles, Ph.D., for their ongoing support of my research and writing. None of this work would be possible without the fantastic support of the Bishop Payne Library staff. The publication of this book coincides with the retirement of Mitzi Budde, D.Min., Head Librarian of Virginia Theological Seminary for over thirty-three years. You will be missed! As always, I am thankful for the support of my parents and for Todd. Most of all, I am deeply grateful to God for inspiration, creativity, and perseverance.

ABBREVIATIONS

1549BCP   Book of Common Prayer, 1549 in Cummings, *The Book of Common Prayer: The Texts of 1549, 1559, and 1662*, 2011.

1552BCP   Book of Common Prayer, 1552 in Cummings, *The Book of Common Prayer: The Texts of 1549, 1559, and 1662*, 2011.

1662BCP   Book of Common Prayer, 1662 in Cummings, *The Book of Common Prayer: The Texts of 1549, 1559, and 1662*, 2011.

1979BCP   *The Book of Common Prayer . . . according to the Use of the Episcopal Church*, 1979.

BEM   *Baptism, Eucharist and Ministry*. Geneva: World Council of Churches, 1982.

INTRODUCTION

From its beginning, the Church has practiced two central rites: baptism and the Eucharist. Between these two rites is an indissoluble bond through which baptism prepares for the Eucharist, and the Eucharist contextualizes baptism. This indissoluble bond also exists with the Church. On the one hand, the Church has formed baptism and the Eucharist through its ritual practice, theology, and canon law. On the other hand, baptism and the Eucharist have formed the Church as the center of its life.

The practice of communion without baptism has become more prevalent within The Episcopal Church.[1] One study suggests that almost twenty-five percent of bishops in The Episcopal Church reported that parishes within their diocese permit communion without baptism.[2] While the canons of The Episcopal Church allow only baptized Christians to receive communion, and a resolution at the 2006 General Convention affirmed this position, a significant number of Episcopal parishes nevertheless continue this practice.[3]

How important, though, is the ordering of these rites? Must baptism be a prerequisite for the reception of communion? How would communion without baptism affect the ecclesiology of The

---

1. For an overview of the issue, see Bogert-Winkler, "The Open Debate on Open Communion in The Episcopal Church." Also, this book uses the current title, The Episcopal Church, even when speaking historically before that title was officially authorized.

2. The Report from the Task Force on "Communion Before Baptism" of the Episcopal Diocese of Northern California as cited in Peterson, "Font to Table or Table to Font?" 46.

3. "No unbaptized person shall be eligible to receive Holy Communion in this Church." The Canons of the Episcopal Church (Title 1.17.7). See also, "Acts of General Convention D084."

Episcopal Church? In this book, we will show that because baptism and the Eucharist form an indissoluble bond that makes the Church, the continued practice of communion without baptism jeopardizes the baptismal-eucharistic ecclesiology of The Episcopal Church.

In chapter one, we will begin by discussing Jesus' table fellowship and its relationship to the Eucharist. Then, in chapter two, we will show the dynamic interplay between baptism, the Eucharist, and the Church throughout church history. Chapter three will show that the 1979 Book of Common Prayer (BCP) of The Episcopal Church expresses a baptismal-eucharistic liturgical theology. Chapter four will articulate a baptismal-eucharistic ecclesiology as the most robust ecclesiology for The Episcopal Church. Finally, the last chapter will describe the relationship between baptism and the Eucharist in other ecclesial communities and show that the continued practice of communion without baptism would jeopardize The Episcopal Church's ecumenical relationships with them. Each chapter also includes a "Diving Deeper" section in which the methodology employed in that chapter will be discussed further.

Setting Some Parameters

The term "communion without baptism" is used for specific reasons. Some use the term "open communion" or "open table" in this discussion. However, these terms are too easily confused with an ongoing debate about opening communion to persons who are not members of one's ecclesial body.[4] This vital issue came before The Episcopal Church in the mid-twentieth century, and the result was that all baptized Christians should be permitted to receive Holy

---

4. For example, as in the Roman Catholic Church, Eastern Orthodox Churches, and the Lutheran Church – Missouri Synod.

Communion.[5] The term "communion before baptism" represents the desire of some to use communion for missiological purposes that will lead the communicant to baptism. However, as chapters four and five will explain, this perspective does not recognize the indissoluble bond between baptism and the Eucharist, which makes the Church. Thus, "communion without baptism" is the most descriptive term.

Because baptism and the Eucharist are central to the life of the Church, they occupy large amounts of scholarship. By necessity, we need to limit the scope of this work. First, this book will reflect primarily on ecclesiology. The arguments used by proponents of communion without baptism are primarily soteriological and missiological. While such arguments do impinge on ecclesiology, they do not address it directly. The ecclesiological implications need to be highlighted, as any change in these rites affects the very integrity of the Church itself.

Furthermore, this book primarily focuses on The Episcopal Church. Chapter two will discuss the dynamic interplay between baptism, the Eucharist, and the Church throughout Church history. Necessarily, that discussion will begin long before The Episcopal Church. However, it will highlight the historical trajectories that led to the current debate within The Episcopal Church. Since these issues are essential for other ecclesial communities, chapter five will discuss the ecclesiological implications from an ecumenical perspective.

Table to Font

Among the many who have called for a change in the traditional practice are careful scholars, knowledgeable theologians, compassionate priests and pastors, and active disciples of Christ. Their contributions to this

---

5. Please see chapter two below for more details.

conversation raise an essential critique of the status quo. While the individual positions are nuanced, they fall into four general categories: Scripture, history, liturgical experience, and theology.

All the proponents of communion without baptism reference Scripture, most notably the feeding narratives of Christ. For example, in his *Let Every Soul Be Jesus' Guest*, Mark Stamm spends an entire chapter on "The Meals of Jesus."[6] In this chapter, he points out that Jesus habitually ate with "sinners and publicans." Stamm also refers to St. Paul's exhortation to the Galatians that, in Christ, they are no longer divided but are to live inclusive lives. He rightfully points out that baptism is how Christians enter the inclusive life of the Church.[7] Therefore, Stamm emphasizes that the welcome to the table before the font is an exception to the "baptismal norm" rather than an attempt to negate it.[8]

Arthur Cochrane provides abundant Scriptural references in his argument in favor of not just communion without baptism but a wholesale reformation of the Lord's Supper. Cochrane suggests that the Church should reunite the Lord's Supper and the Agape Meal mentioned in 1 Corinthians 11.[9] He advocates for a return to a full meal, including meat, poultry, and pork, as a sign of the abundant spirit that should accompany the Lord's Supper. He also reminds the Church of the connection between the Eucharist and *diakonia* (service to the poor).[10] Through "corporate act[s] of *diakonia*," he argues that the Church reunites the Lord's Supper with the Agape Meal ethically and missionally.

---

6. Stamm, *Let Every Soul be Jesus' Guest*, 41.
7. Stamm, *Let Every Soul be Jesus' Guest*, 48.
8. Stamm, *Let Every Soul be Jesus' Guest*, 61.
9. Cochrane, *Eating and Drinking with Jesus*, 78.
10. Cochrane, *Eating and Drinking with Jesus*, 89.

Richard Fabian also looks to Scripture in his promotion of communion without baptism.[11] He helpfully points out that John the Baptist and members of the community of Essenes in Jesus' day emphasized ritual purity as a sign of eschatological witness. They urged their fellow Israelites to perform numerous ritual cleansings to prepare for the "day of the Lord." Fabian then argues that Jesus abandoned baptism and instead chose an inclusive meal practice as his preferred means of signifying the reign of God. These narratives, he argues, lead to the conclusion that Jesus welcomed tax collectors and sinners to the table. Similarly, the Church should not distinguish between the "pure" and the "impure" when welcoming people to the eucharistic table.[12]

In addition to Scripture, Fabian also appeals to history. He rightly points to the diminishment of communion during the fifth century when adults would postpone their baptism almost to the point of death.[13] As discussed in chapter two, the Church has long struggled with narrowing baptism to a purity rite. Therefore, Fabian's critique of the narrow view of baptism as a rite allowing only the "pure" to receive communion is laudable. Stamm also utilizes history to appeal to Wesley's reference to the Eucharist as a "converting ordinance."[14] He suggests that Wesley opened the opportunity for an "exception" to the catholic Ordo by recognizing the Eucharist's potential to convert sinners. Chapter three discusses the Ordo, and chapter five discusses the idea of the Eucharist as a "converting ordinance."

Some proponents of communion without baptism appeal to liturgical experience as support for their position. In her moving

---

11. Fabian, "First the Table, then the Font," n.p.
12. Fabian, "First the Table, then the Font," n.p.
13. Fabian, "First the Table, then the Font," n.p.
14. Stamm, *Let Every Soul be Jesus' Guest*, 63.

autobiography *Take This Bread*, Sara Miles shares her conversion story when receiving communion at St. Gregory of Nyssa in San Francisco.[15] She speaks of her parents raising her as an atheist quite intentionally and how she became very active in social justice issues worldwide, particularly as a reporter. One day, she walked into St. Gregory's and participated in the eucharistic service. When the person beside her handed her a portion of bread and said, "This is the Body of Christ," her entire life changed. With time, she became quite active at St. Gregory's. Miles put Cochrane's exhortation that the Lord's Supper ought to be an expression of *diakonia* to work quite literally by starting a food pantry that used the Lord's Table to distribute to the poor.[16] Of course, as a clergyperson at St. Gregory's, Fabian also echoes this appeal to their liturgical experience.[17]

Stephen Edmonson considers liturgical experience as the primary source of theological consideration.[18] He argues that because the practice of communion without baptism comes from the grassroots experiences of local parishes, it constitutes a "first-order theology" that should supersede later theological reflection.[19] He bases this argument on his interpretation of the liturgical maxim *lex orandi, lex credendi*. Chapter three looks more carefully at his arguments.

In her critique of an earlier essay by James Farwell, Kathryn Tanner offers theological arguments in favor of communion without baptism.[20] Like Stamm, she points to Jesus' inclusive meal practices

---

15. Miles, *Take This Bread*, 54.
16. Miles, *Take This Bread*, 119.
17. Fabian, "First the Table, then the Font."
18. Edmonson, "Opening the Table," 214.
19. Edmonson, "Opening the Table," 214.
20. Tanner, "In Praise of Open Communion," 475-477.

as justification for a change in traditional practice. Additionally, she helpfully points out that the qualities that distinguish God's reign are its inclusiveness and openness.[21] She also critiques Farwell's position that contemporary "unchurched" persons seek communion without baptism due to their desire for immediate gratification.[22] As mentioned above, the Church should not use baptism to measure the strength of a person's desire to follow Christ. As Tanner comments, enough obstacles exist in the modern world that can prevent and distract people from Christ without baptism being included.

Finally, Karl Barth systematically appraises baptism in his essay *The Teaching of the Church Regarding Baptism*. He also speaks briefly about baptism and the Lord's Supper in his unpublished final volume of *Church Dogmatics* IV, 4. Most of Barth's work focuses on the soteriological aspects of baptism. Nonetheless, Barth helpfully reminds the Church that baptism is not ultimately about salvation, receiving the Holy Spirit, or initiation into the Church but is primarily about giving glory to God through Christ.[23] Barth questions the ordering of baptism. He distinguishes between baptism's inherent nature and divine power and the Church's ordering.[24] However, Barth does not suggest reordering the Ordo: "Baptism in particular refers to the foundation of the Christian life, and the Lord's Supper to its renewal."[25] He wishes to clearly distinguish between the purpose of baptism, the Lord's Supper, and the Church's administration of them. Barth continues by refuting the claims that baptism and the Lord's Supper are in any way mediations of God's grace or even sacraments.

---

21. Tanner, "In Praise of Open Communion," 479.
22. Tanner, "In Praise of Open Communion," 480.
23. Barth, *The Teaching of the Church Regarding Baptism*, 30–31.
24. Barth, *The Teaching of the Church Regarding Baptism*, 34.
25. Barth, *The Christian Life*, 45.

For Barth, they are "actions of human obedience."[26] Barth is correct in recognizing that the Church ultimately baptizes in obedience to our Lord's express commandment, not because the Church can somehow constrain God's grace to operate solely through baptism or any other sacraments.

Proponents of communion without baptism correctly critique baptism solely as a purity rite. In the subsequent chapters, we will show that the Church is most faithful when it teaches a full and rich understanding of baptism. Also, God freely acts in any manner to bring reconciliation to humanity. While the sacraments are a true and faithful sign of God's grace, they should never be considered a constraint on God's redeeming work. Finally, pastoral situations arise in which a rigid adherence to the traditional Ordo would be inappropriate and detrimental to the Gospel.

Proponents of communion without baptism are correct on these critical issues but are incorrect in their proposed methodology to address them. A public and permanent change to the traditional Ordo is not warranted. Such a change would have devastating consequences for the ecclesiology of The Episcopal Church. This book argues that The Episcopal Church is most faithful to the Gospel of God's redeeming work through Christ when it recognizes the indissoluble bond between baptism, the Eucharist, and the Church.

---

26. Barth, *The Christian Life*, 46.

CHAPTER ONE

JESUS' TABLE FELLOWSHIP, BAPTISM, AND THE EUCHARIST

As mentioned above, proponents of communion without baptism use Scripture extensively in their argument for changing the traditional Ordo.[1] They claim that the narratives of Jesus' table fellowship support the practice of communion without baptism. For example, Tanner rightfully emphasizes the radical hospitality that Jesus exhibited during his ministry to those persons deemed sinners and religiously impure by the Jewish authorities of that time.[2] She and other proponents of communion without baptism interpret these narratives as justification for making the sacramental grace of the Eucharist available to all people and not only to baptized Christians. Just as Christ opened his table to all people, they argue, so should the Church open the eucharistic table to all people.[3]

In this chapter, we will critique the use of Scriptural references to Jesus' table fellowship in support of communion without baptism by considering their canonical context. First, we will explain how the

---

1. This chapter is an updated and expanded version of Shawn Strout, "Jesus' Table Fellowship, Baptism, and the Eucharist," *The Anglican Theological Review* 98, no. 3 (Sum 2016): 479-934.

2. Tanner, "In Praise of Open Communion," 475-477.

3. Tanner, "In Praise of Open Communion"; Edmonson, "Opening the Table," 218; Fabian, "First the Table, then the Font"; and Stamm, *Let Every Soul be Jesus' Guest*, 45.

canonical context of those Scriptural passages argues in favor of the traditional Ordo rather than for a change to it. Then, we will provide an example of how canonical context intensifies the radical hospitality called for by proponents of communion without baptism using the traditional Ordo rather than changing it.

The Canonical Context Explained

If considered solely as literal narratives of the historical Jesus, then these feeding stories of Jesus might give an account that could support the practice of communion without baptism. However, when considered from a canonical perspective, these narratives speak to and within the eucharistic communities of baptized believers.[4] Thus, instead of advocating communion without baptism, these narratives, considered within their canonical context, reinvigorate the indissoluble bond between baptism and the Eucharist, which forms the Church.

To understand the context of these narratives, we will begin with the canonical shaping of the New Testament. While the Gospel narratives are placed at the beginning of the New Testament, they are not its oldest books. Biblical scholars today generally agree that the letters written by Paul are the oldest extant Christian writings, with First Thessalonians being the oldest.[5] While Paul does not write about baptism or the Eucharist in First Thessalonians, he does write about baptism in Galatians, his following letter in our present-day canon, which was written around 55 C.E.[6] In Galatians 3, Paul speaks about the relationship between the Law and faith. He is attempting

---

4. For an exposition on canonical hermeneutics, see Childs, *Introduction to the Old Testament as Scripture*, 69-106.

5. Brown, *An Introduction to the New Testament*, 456.

6. Brown, *An Introduction to the New Testament*, 468.

to persuade the Church at Galatia that faith in Christ will fulfill all the requirements of the Law. Then, in verse twenty-seven, he states, "As many of you as were baptized into Christ have clothed yourselves with Christ."[7] Ferguson provides a vital interpretation of Paul's view of the relationship between faith and baptism:

> Paul binds faith and baptism together as two aspects of entering into Christ. One now belongs to Christ on the basis of faith in him by being baptized into him. If a distinction is to be made between the relation of faith and baptism to the blessings described, one might say that baptism is the time at which and faith is the reason why.[8]

While Ferguson suggests a temporal connection between baptism and faith, the metaphorical imagery also points out a spatial connection. Paul describes the Galatians as being "baptized *into* Christ." This metaphor indicates a type of spatial entry. At one point, the Galatians were outside Christ, but now they are in Christ. For Paul, both faith and baptism provide that entrance *into* Christ.

A couple of years after writing to the Galatians, Paul wrote his first letter to the Church at Corinth in late 56 C.E. to early 57 C.E.[9] In this letter, he treats baptism and the Eucharist in much greater detail. For example, in 1 Corinthians 10, Paul instructs the Corinthian Church on how to behave during the Eucharist. First, he recalls the Exodus narrative in which God, through Moses, leads the people of Israel out of Egypt through the Red Sea and into the wilderness, where God then provides them manna from the sky and water to drink from a rock. Paul likens the

---

7. All scripture quotations are taken from the *New Revised Standard Version* of the Bible.
8. Ferguson, *Baptism in the Early Church*, 147.
9. Brown, *An Introduction to the New Testament*, 512.

Israelites crossing the Red Sea to baptism, eating manna and drinking from the rock to the Eucharist. The movement through the Red Sea and the supply of manna and water are similar to being "baptized *into* Christ." Paul sees a progression from baptism to the Eucharist.

However, what is most interesting is that he does not demonstrate a need to spell this out specifically for the Corinthians. Thus, LaVerdiere suggests, "From Paul's presentation, we see how baptism and the Eucharist were very closely related in both life and theology."[10] This close relationship is evident because Paul finds explicitly stating it unnecessary. At this early time in the Church, the movement of baptism to the Eucharist must have been so ingrained in the ritual consciousness of the early Church that it was utterly unnecessary to refer to this chronological and spatial movement specifically.

Paul not only relates closely baptism and the Eucharist, but he also speaks specifically about their ecclesiological implications. In verses 16 and 17, he writes, "The cup of blessing that we bless, is it not a sharing in the blood of Christ? The bread that we break, is it not a sharing in the body of Christ? Because there is one bread, we who are many are one body, for we all partake of the one bread." Paul is not speaking of individual participation in the Eucharist but corporate participation in the Church. Thus, for Paul, the Eucharist and the Church are closely related.

In 1 Corinthians 11, he continues by chiding the Church at Corinth for the divisions that persist in their community right up to and during the celebration of the Eucharist (vv. 17-22). He tells them that he cannot commend them for this behavior. Instead, he exhorts them with those words he has received from the Lord Jesus and has handed them to them. Then, he moves into what later will be known as the Institution Narrative found in nearly every Eucharistic

---

10. LaVerdiere, *The Eucharist in the New Testament and the Early Church*, 37.

Prayer.[11] Finally, he speaks of those who partake of the Eucharist unworthily. Paul's juxtaposition of first division within the Church, the reminder of what will later be known as the Institution Narrative, and the exhortation to partake of the Eucharist worthily are essential.

Kilmartin contends that, for Paul, these elements are inherently connected. To partake of the Eucharist unworthily is to fail to see the inherent connection between the Eucharist and the Church. Kilmartin makes this connection when he states, "Having failed to observe fraternal charity which was demanded of Christians, they also failed to recognize that the Christ they received is not merely the Christ-for-me but the Christ-for-many. . . Therefore, 'without distinguishing the body' equals *without recognizing the Eucharistic body in its specific claim to fraternal charity* [italics in original]."[12] Michael Welker also argues that the wealthy Corinthians were not sharing the food with the poor: "This is what constitutes the 'unworthiness' of the way in which the meal is celebrated! Instead of demonstrating mutual acceptance and justice in the celebration of the Supper, the perverted meal becomes a sign and demonstration of inequality and injustice!"[13]

In 1 Corinthians 10, Paul speaks of a close relationship between baptism and the Eucharist. In 1 Corinthians 11, he speaks of the close relationship between the Eucharist and the Church. Again, this progression of baptism to the Eucharist to the Church is natural for Paul. He does not stress the order of these events. Instead, his emphasis is on their theological significance.

Paul understands the close relationship between baptism, the Eucharist, and the Church, but what does this understanding have

---

11. The Anaphora of Addai and Mara does not contain the Institution Narrative.

12. Kilmartin, *The Eucharist in the Primitive Church*, 88.

13. Welker, *What Happens in Holy Communion?*, 78. See also Hofius, "Herrenmahl und Herrenmahlsparadosis: Erwagungen zu 1 Kor 11, 23b-25," 220.

to do with the narratives of Jesus' table fellowship found in the Gospels? Because Paul's epistles were written before the Gospels, they demonstrate the theological *Sitz im Leben* in which the Gospels were written.[14] The present task is to place the narratives of Jesus' table fellowship within their proper historical and canonical context.

While not about table fellowship, one narrative that all four Gospels share is the account of Jesus' baptism. This story precedes all other narratives regarding Jesus' ministry except for his birth and early childhood. A natural progression from Jesus' baptism into his public ministry is evident. None of the table fellowship narratives occur before these narratives of Jesus' baptism.

However, is Jesus' baptism equivalent to baptism in the Church? If baptism is meant for the remission of sins as found in the Apostles' and Nicene Creeds, then what does that mean for Jesus, who is said to be without sin (Hebrews 4:15)? Was Jesus' baptism completely different from later Christian baptism, or are there parallels between them? Even though the details of Jesus' baptism differ in the four narratives, two features remain the same: the coming of the Holy Spirit as a dove, with the voice from heaven declaring him "Son" and the mention of the future baptism in the Holy Spirit. Therefore, as Ferguson argues, Jesus' baptism is similar to Christian baptism through adoption as children of God and reception of the Holy Spirit.[15] Jesus' baptism acts as the root of Christian baptism.

Furthermore, Johnson identifies two references from the Hebrew Scriptures in the pronouncement from the Father during Jesus' baptism. They come from Psalm 2:7, which is meant for the coronation of kings, and Isaiah 42:1, which is about the calling of

---

14. See the Diving Deeper section for more details.
15. Ferguson, *Baptism in the Early Church*, 101-103.

the "Suffering Servant."[16] Johnson concludes that the divine voice at Jesus' baptism is not calling a great and powerful Messiah but a "suffering Messiah." He states, "In this way, then, scholars have seen this baptismal event at the Jordan as having 'vocational' significance for Jesus' own life and ministry."[17] Thus, Jesus' baptism is not about purity from sin but rather a vocation for ministry.

Similarly, later Christian baptism is primarily about vocation for ministry, not purity from sin. Therefore, proponents of communion without baptism are correct in critiquing baptism as solely a purity rite. Baptism involves much more than the remission of sins. Chapter two will highlight, through the course of Church history, many discussions regarding the connection between baptism, the Holy Spirit, and ministerial vocation, which will have important implications for ecclesiology.

The proper context for the narratives of Jesus' public ministry is evident. In all four Gospels, Jesus' baptism precedes his public ministry. Furthermore, Paul's epistles precede all four Gospels. In his epistles, he assumes that baptism precedes the Eucharist. Without this context, misunderstandings can occur regarding Jesus' table fellowship narratives.

In many instances, Jesus shared table fellowship with those the religious establishment deemed inappropriate (Matthew 9, 11; Mark 2; Luke 5, 7). Furthermore, all four Gospel narratives give the account of the "Feeding of the Five Thousand" (Matthew 14, Mark 6, Luke 9, and John 6), and Matthew and Mark go even further by giving another account of the "Feeding of the Four Thousand" (Matthew 15 and Mark 8). These narratives aptly describe Jesus' generosity in seeking all who are hungry and lost.

Stamm argues that these feeding stories are about the Eucharist. He points out the four-fold eucharistic shape found in the feeding

---

16. Johnson, *The Rites of Christian Initiation*, 16.
17. Johnson, *The Rites of Christian Initiation*.

stories of Mark 6 and Luke 9 and Paul's shipwreck in Malta in Acts 27.[18] He and others[19] have suggested that these narratives support the practice of communion without baptism. They argue that, because Jesus had an open table fellowship, so should the Church.

To use these narratives in this fashion is to forget the context in which they were written and read. Early Christians very likely read these narratives in the context of the Eucharist, just as contemporary Christians read them in that same context today. Thus, that liturgical context would have impacted their interpretation of the narratives.

For LaVerdiere, these narratives are explanations of the role of the Eucharist in the Church. For example, he suggests that the ten meal narratives found in Luke each show a distinct purpose for the Eucharist. The feast with Levi (5:27-39) shows the need for repentance. The breaking of bread at Bethsaida (9:10-17) shows the mission of the Church, and so they continue.[20] Their primary point is not to describe Christ's historical actions but to speak theologically to the Church.

While proponents of communion without baptism are correct that these feeding stories are eucharistic, they misunderstand the narrative and canonical context of these stories when they suggest these stories support the practice of communion without baptism. McGowan aptly states, "If we accept the form-critical approach that the Gospels were written within the milieu of early Christian communities, then we must also recognize this in the case of Jesus' meal practices."[21] Otherwise, the Church runs the risk of suggesting that the Gospel narratives' primary purpose is to provide readers with a literal, historical

---

18. Stamm, *Let Every Soul be Jesus' Guest*, 45. Note: Stamm does go on to recognize the ecclesial context in which these narratives were written, cf. 54-55.

19. Cf. Kathryn Tanner, "In Praise of Open Communion," 476-477; Edmonson, "Opening the Table," 218.

20. LaVerdiere, *The Eucharist in the New Testament and the Early Church*, 83-94.

21. McGowan, "The Meals of Jesus and the Meals of the Church," 111.

account of the life of Jesus rather than the understanding of the life of Jesus as seen through the lens of the diverse communities of faith to whom and in whom these narratives were written.

While the narratives of Jesus' table fellowship may be eucharistic, the Institution Narratives themselves (Matt. 26:26-29, Mark 14:22-25, Luke 22:19-20, and 1 Cor. 11:23-25) are explicitly so. Again, the question of context arises. Much debate exists about the historical situation of the Institution Narratives. Some suggest that the Institution Narrative found in most Eucharistic Prayers[22] originates in the historical Last Supper.[23] Others suggest nearly the opposite—that the Gospel narrative of the Last Supper originated in the liturgical practice of the Lord's Supper.[24] Others believe that no correlation exists either way.[25] Did the historical account of the Last Supper give rise to the rite of the Lord's Supper? Or did the practice of the Lord's Supper in the early Church influence the development of the narrative of the Last Supper? A definitive answer remains elusive. However, a strong connection did exist between the rite of the Lord's Supper and the narrative of the Last Supper.

In the canonical shaping of Scripture, baptism and the Eucharist play a central role in the feeding narratives of Jesus. In the next section, we will consider an example of a narrative that proponents of communion without baptism often cite to support their claim that baptism need not precede communion. By looking carefully at the canonical shaping of this narrative, we will show that this narrative reinforces baptism before communion rather than its alternative.

---

22. Although absent from one of the earliest extant Eucharistic liturgies found in the *Didache*. See Bradshaw, *Eucharistic Origins*, 26-27.
23. Kilmartin, 28.
24. LaVerdiere, 23.
25. Bradshaw, *Reconstructing Early Christian Worship*, 10.

The Canonical Context Exemplified

The narrative of the Syrophoenician woman in Mark 7:24-30 provides an example of Jesus' radical hospitality toward the outcast. We will examine this passage within its Markan context and its relationship to Pauline texts and the late-first-century document the *Didache*. These examinations will reveal the author of Mark's intention to critique the eucharistic practices of the apostolic Church. However, we will also argue that the suggestion that this critique of eucharistic practice extends to eliminating baptism before communion would nullify the central theme of Mark—identification with Christ as the Crucified-Risen One.

Mark 7:24-30 tells the story of the Syrophoenician woman's attempt to have Jesus heal her daughter. At this point in the narrative, Jesus has left Galilee and entered Tyre, Gentile territory. He enters a house and does not wish anyone to know he is there. Nonetheless, a woman, whose daughter has an unclean spirit, follows him into the house. She drops to Jesus' feet and begs him to save her daughter. Jesus responds with an answer that proves shocking to the modern-day ear: "Let the children be fed first, for it is not fair to take the children's food and throw it to the dogs (Mark 7:27)." Just as today, calling a person a "dog" was a grave insult.[26] Furthermore, Jesus appears to be tying this insult to the woman's ethnicity as a Gentile. Undaunted, the woman replies, "Sir, even the dogs under the table eat the children's crumbs (7:28)." Jesus responds to her faithfulness by healing her daughter of the unclean spirit.

Read out of context, this passage appears to have little to commend it. At best, it displays Jesus' human side with glaring clarity. However, a closer look at this narrative's intra-Markan, inter-canonical, and

---

26. Theissen, *The Gospels in Context*, 61-62.

historical contexts reveals Mark's intention to critique the eucharistic practice of the early Church. We will first consider this narrative within its intra-Markan context.

In his book *The Four Gospels on Sunday*, Gordon Lathrop suggests that the author of Mark uses a series of circles, or chiasms, to provide rhetorical parallelisms for emphasis. These parallelisms walk the reader through a series of narratives through which the author unfolds a larger message for the reader. Thus, the author uses the entire sequence of parallelisms to convey a meaning that each narrative independently cannot convey. The center of the sequence represents the author's most important message. In this case, the narrative of the Syrophoenician woman marks the center of these feeding narratives (Mark 6:6b-13 - Mark 8:14-21):

> A Sending of the Twelve without bread—6:6b-13
>   B Herod's meal, return of the disciples—6:14-30
>   C Feeding of the five thousand—6:31-44
>   D Walking on the sea and healing—6:45-56
>   E *Controversy with Pharisees on purity*
>   *. . . In the house: all food clean*
>   *. . . In the house at Tyre: crumbs from the table for all*—7:1-30
>   D' Ephphatha—7:31-37
>   C' Feeding of the four thousand—8:1-10
>   B' The Pharisees seek a sign from heaven—8:11-13
> A' The disciples have no bread: the yeast and the baskets full—8:14-21[27]

Passages A, B, C, and D occur within Jewish territory, while passages D', C', B', and A' occur within Gentile territory.

---

27. Lathrop, *The Four Gospels on Sunday*, 77.

As the center of the chiasm, passage E is the hinge for this narrative sequence and thus provides the author's central intention for the chiasm. Passage E begins with Mark 7:1-23, which describes yet another confrontation between Jesus and the Pharisees. The Pharisees have criticized Jesus because his disciples do not wash properly before eating. Jesus returns the critique by quoting Isaiah 29:13 from the Septuagint: "This people honors me with their lips, but their hearts are far from me; in vain do they worship me, teaching human precepts as doctrines (Mark 7:6-7)." Jesus explains to the crowd that it is not what enters the body that defiles the body but what comes from the heart.

Then, Jesus enters a house (Mark 7:17). Lathrop recognizes a pattern in Mark where Jesus shares a general teaching with the crowd but then interprets it to the disciples usually in a house. Because the gospel of Mark itself would have been proclaimed within the liturgy of the house churches, Lathrop makes a compelling argument that the author of Mark uses houses as a rhetorical device to indicate the Church.[28] Accepting this hermeneutical key, the reader can then presume that the author of Mark wishes to get the Church's attention with this narrative by means of his reference to the house. From the beginning of this series of feeding stories in 6:6b-13 to this point in the narrative, Jesus has not entered a single house. Now, he enters a house. And now, the author of Mark speaks directly to the Church. The author of Mark uses Jesus' teaching against the Pharisees' overemphasis upon ritual purification generally to critique the Church's overemphasis upon ritual purification in the assembly. Through this symbolic use of "house," the author of Mark wishes to reform the eucharistic practice of the Church.

Jesus leaves this house and enters another house. Again, the author of Mark wishes to draw the attention of the Church to the

---

28. Lathrop, *The Four Gospels on Sunday*, 68.

following narrative. The Syrophoenician woman enters after Jesus and throws herself at his feet. Historically, a woman, and a Gentile woman at that, would not enter a strange house and throw herself at the feet of a strange man lest she risk her reputation. However, Lathrop's hermeneutical key regarding Mark's use of houses signifies a deeper message here. The author of Mark is addressing the presence of Gentiles within the Church. Furthermore, the imagery of bread on the table has strong eucharistic overtones. The author of Mark is telling the apostolic Church not only to allow Gentiles into the Church but to allow them access to the eucharistic table. Coupled with Christ's declaration of all food as clean in the passage above, this passage declares all persons clean.

Thus, proponents of communion without baptism are right that Jesus' feeding narratives generally and this narrative specifically argue for reform of the eucharistic practices of the Church. All persons, regardless of gender or ethnic identity, should have access to the eucharistic table. However, a closer examination of the Pauline context of this narrative and its relationship to the late-first-century text the *Didache* reveals that this critique does not extend to baptism, as that would nullify the very purpose of Mark's gospel—identification with Christ as the Crucified-Risen One.

Scholars have long debated the influence of Pauline theology upon the author of Mark. For a time, the question appeared to be answered. However, more recent scholarship is once again raising it.[29] Lathrop suggests that the occasion for the writing of Mark may have been the death of Paul in the Neronian persecutions, based on evidence in the *First Letter of Clement*.[30] Due to limited space, we will not trace all the commonalities between Pauline theology and

---

29. Marcus, "Mark – Interpreter of Paul," 473–474.
30. Lathrop, *The Four Gospels on Sunday*, 21-22.

Mark. Instead, we will focus on the common theology of the cross that they share, as emphasized by Joel Marcus: "Both Paul and Mark lay *extraordinary* stress on the death of Jesus."[31] Marcus provides a number of examples that elucidate this emphasis upon *theologia crucis* (theology of the cross) in Paul and Mark as an unpopular theme in the early Church.[32] Thus, Lathrop believes Mark's intention was to critique the assemblies for their lack of focus upon Christ as the Crucified-Risen One in their midst.[33]

Lathrop's chiastic structure for the feeding narratives in Mark 6:6b—8:21 focuses upon this critique. As mentioned above, the hinge in the chiasm is the narrative of the Syrophoenician woman. From this point forward, the narratives occur in Gentile territory. Therefore, the narrative regarding the feeding of the four thousand becomes more than a mere repetition of the previous narrative of the feeding of the five thousand. Instead, the feeding of the four thousand continues Mark's critique of eucharistic practice. Located within Gentile territory, this narrative focuses on the inclusion of Gentiles in the eucharistic meal.

Charles Bobertz draws an important parallel between Jesus' statement in 8:2 and his death:

> [The crowd has] been with Jesus for three days in his death. It is this last symbolic level which is at the heart of Mark's rationale for the inclusion of the Gentiles. In Mark's gospel every other use of the expression 'three days' (ἡμέραι τρέις) has to do with the period of Jesus in the tomb, that is, he will rise after three days (Mark 8:31; 9:3; 10:34; 14:50:15:29). The

---

31. Lathrop, *The Four Gospels on Sunday*, 479.
32. Lathrop, *The Four Gospels on Sunday*, 481-484.
33. Lathrop, *The Four Gospels on Sunday*, 72-73.

easiest reading of the narrative on a symbolic level, therefore, is that these Gentiles rightfully belong at the ritual eucharist, and therefore resurrection, because they have entered into the death of Christ (presumably through an implied ritual baptism).[34]

Thus, according to Bobertz's proposal, this three-day imagery stands in for baptism in this narrative. Using this expression, the author of Mark draws the connection between baptism, identification with Christ's death and burial, and the subsequent eucharistic meal. Therefore, the author of Mark is not attempting to critique baptism before the Eucharist but rather is drawing attention to baptism, not as a purity rite, but as participation in Christ as the Crucified-Risen One.

Another critique of eucharistic practice in this chiastic structure occurs in Mark 8:14-21. In his lecture on January 24, 2012, Lathrop drew an important connection between Mark's mention of the "yeast of the Pharisees and the yeast of Herod" (8:15) with Paul's rebuke of the Corinthian's eucharistic practice in 1 Corinthians 11. Mark's mention of "the yeast of the Pharisees" is a rebuke of ritual purity as a prerequisite for eucharistic practice as pictured in the narrative of the Syrophoenician woman. Likewise, his mention of "the yeast of Herod" is a rebuke of the oppression of the rich over the poor. Paul makes a similar rebuke in 1 Corinthians 11, where he admonishes the Corinthian church for its unequal treatment of the rich and the poor (11:21). The Eucharist is not the place for such divisions. The table should be open to all, regardless of socio-economic status.

However, this openness to all does not circumvent baptism. As proposed above, the narrative of the feeding of the four thousand

---

34. Bobertz, "Ritual Eucharist Within Narrative," 96.

includes a reference to baptismal identification with the Crucified-Risen One in their midst. Furthermore, Paul speaks of the flow of baptism to the Eucharist in 1 Corinthians 10, just before his rebuke of their eucharistic practices. In 10:1-5, he draws analogies of baptism with the Israelites' crossing of the Jordan and of the Eucharist with their subsequent feeding on manna in the wilderness (10:1-5). Paul makes another connection between baptism and the death and burial of Christ in Romans 6:4, and the author of Colossians, influenced by Pauline theology, makes a similar connection in Colossians 2:12. While the eucharistic table is open to all persons, regardless of gender, ethnicity, or socio-economic status, that openness remains predicated upon identification with Christ as the Crucified-Risen One through baptism. This identification with Christ is not a privilege or a badge of honor to lord over others. Rather, it is identification with Christ, who in turn identifies with the outcasts.

Bobertz suggests that the entire gospel of Mark focuses on the inclusion of the Gentiles at the eucharistic table. However, Bobertz claims that Mark does not argue for the presence of Gentiles based on purification rites. In fact, Mark argues quite to the contrary. Instead, as Bobertz states, "[W]hat characterizes the presentation of the rituals of baptism and eucharist in *Mark* is the strong association of the liminal space of ritual with the death of Christ."[35] Thus, Mark does not view baptism as a purification rite but as identification with Christ as the Crucified-Risen One. Any attempt to eliminate baptism before communion would nullify Mark's intention to justify the inclusion of the Gentiles at the eucharistic table *because of* their identification with Christ as the Crucified-Risen One in baptism.

Mark's baptismal theology based upon a *theologia crucis* rather than upon purification becomes important in considering the

---

35. Bobertz, "Ritual Eucharist Within Narrative," 95.

late-first-century text, the *Didache*. The *Didache* is one of the earliest liturgical sources available, possibly written contemporaneously with the later books of the New Testament. Flusser suggests that the author of the *Didache* may have used an earlier Jewish source called *The Two Ways* for much of the preliminary material. He believes this earlier material would have been contemporary with the early apostolic Church. In fact, the author of the *Didache* may have believed it to have apostolic origin.[36]

In chapter seven, the *Didache* gives a detailed description of the baptismal rite. Then, in chapter nine, it quite forcefully prohibits the communication of the unbaptized: "9.5 Let no one eat or drink of your thanksgiving [meal] save those who have been baptized in the name of the Lord, since the Lord has said concerning this, 'Do not give what is holy to dogs.'"[37] The exact nature of this "thanksgiving [meal]" is unknown. For example, the eucharistic liturgy in the *Didache* does not include the Institution Narrative, which is present in most other Eucharistic Prayers.[38] Therefore, some scholars have suggested that the meal it describes is not the Eucharist but rather an *agape* meal. Other scholars suggest it is just an earlier form of the eucharistic liturgy. Bradshaw takes a middle viewpoint by wondering if the *Didache* suggests a diversity of eucharistic practices at that time.[39] Regardless of the exact nature of this meal, the Church or at least some communities within it have developed a more formal norm for the relationship between baptism and this meal, whether it is the Eucharist or another type of meal.

---

36. Flusser, "Paul's Jewish Christian Opponents in the *Didache*," 73-74.
37. "The Didache," 2.
38. Bradshaw, *Eucharistic Origins*, 26-27.
39. Bradshaw, *Eucharistic Origins*, 32.

The *Didache* emphasizes the necessity of baptism before communion. However, the baptismal theology of the *Didache* focuses upon purification as the sole imagery for baptism. Bobertz and Lathrop argue that Mark wishes to critique an overemphasis upon purification, which also appears in the *Didache's* baptismal theology.[40] The narrative of the Syrophoenician woman draws this critique into clarity with its reference to "the dogs." If the *Didache*, or some precursor to it, was indeed a popular writing during the time of Paul and Mark, perhaps this reference speaks directly to the baptismal theology in 9.5. Bobertz makes an insightful connection:

> For the *Didache* separateness and holiness lie at the heart of an alternative universe, that is, the separate physical, social, and theological space created by ritual: 'do not give what is holy to the dogs'. For *Mark* the death of Christ lies at the heart of ritual space, for some who are the participants, especially the Gentiles, find themselves ritually placed within that death in baptism and table-fellowship: 'they have been with me now for three days.'[41]

Mark wishes to reform the current eucharistic practice by declaring that the eucharistic table is open to all people. However, identification with Christ as the Crucified-Risen One, who also identifies with the outcasts, marks that openness. Baptism is the ritual means by which they identify with Christ, not as an act of exclusive superiority but rather as an inclusive identification with all those with whom Christ also identifies.

---

40. Bobertz, "Ritual Eucharist Within Narrative," 95 and Lathrop, *The Four Gospels on Sunday*, 72, respectively.

41. Bobertz, "Ritual Eucharist Within Narrative," 98-99.

Mark's narrative of the Syrophoenician woman provides an important critique of eucharistic practice. The eucharistic table is not reserved only for the wealthy or the ritually pure. It is open to all persons who wish to identify with Christ, the Crucified-Risen One. However, proponents of communion without baptism misunderstand when they suggest that these feeding narratives do not consider baptism as integral to the Eucharist. A close look at the intra-Markan, inter-canonical, and historical contexts of this narrative within its chiastic structure shows that baptism as identification with the Crucified-Risen One is indeed inherent within these texts. The Church will greatly benefit from a critique of the prevailing image of baptism as a purification rite instead of identification with Christ as the Crucified-Risen One. Proponents of communion without baptism are correct in offering this critique. The Church ought never to see baptism as a barrier to communion or as an initiatory hurdle to overcome. Baptism is about identification with Christ, and the Eucharist is about renewed identification with Christ. This expanded imagery of baptism, therefore, reforms the view that the Eucharist is meant only for the pure.[42] Instead, the Eucharist is communion with Christ as the Crucified-Risen One, who welcomes the outcasts, and with whom Christians have identified through baptism.

Diving Deeper

From its inception, the Church has understood Scripture to play a pivotal role in decision-making. It has been and remains an authoritative text. Anglicans have also recognized the importance

---

42. Therefore, a generous pastoral response to newcomers who may just be meeting Christ for the first time in a Eucharistic service is appropriate. Please see the conclusion for pastoral considerations.

of Scripture but allowed for various interpretations. But how do these interpretations occur? And are they all of the same value in determining the doctrine of the Church?

This section will briefly introduce Scriptural hermeneutics, the practice of interpreting Scripture. It will also briefly describe four hermeneutical approaches: historical-grammatical, historical-critical, form-critical, and canonical-critical. Many other hermeneutical forms exist and offer valuable insights into Scripture.[43]

One hermeneutical approach is to interpret Scripture literally. However, this approach is is not feasible. Take Psalm 18:2, for example, "The Lord is my rock, my fortress, and my deliverer, my God, my rock in whom I take refuge, my shield, and the horn of my salvation, my stronghold." If we take this passage literally, the Lord would be six to seven items: rock, fortress/stronghold, deliverer, God, shield, and horn of salvation. Clearly, the psalmist is speaking metaphorically about the Lord.

The historical-grammatical approach seeks to interpret Scripture based on a "plain reading" within its historical context. Thus, the various genres of Scripture must be considered. The psalm quoted above is an example of poetry that uses metaphor, analogy, and hyperbole. Therefore, the careful interpreter would not expect God to be a literal rock or fortress but understands those images as metaphors regarding God's character. Also, the historical context of the stated author and audience would assist in interpretation.

However, this approach makes a few assumptions. First, it assumes that the stated author of the passage is the actual author. Therefore, David wrote the Psalms. Men named Matthew, Mark, Luke, and John wrote the four Gospels. Also, this method assumes that the audience

---

43. For an excellent summary of these three forms and many others, see Knight, *Methods of Biblical Interpretation*.

would have been contemporary to the author. Thus, David wrote to the people of Israel on the day "the Lord delivered him from the hand of all his enemies, and from the hand of Saul (Psalm 18 incipit)."

The grammatical-historical approach stresses the stability of the text from its writing to today. This stability is important because the theological grounding for this approach is the inerrancy of Scripture. God inspired the original authors to write the very words of Scripture and has divinely preserved those words through the ages to this day. Thus, the reader may consider these words the inerrant, inspired Word of God.[44]

While these theological assumptions underlie the conscious use of the historical-grammatical method, readers of Scripture often use this method regardless of these underlying assumptions. For example, a "plain reading" of Scripture assumes that stories in the Gospels of Jesus' table fellowship depict historical events of Jesus. The text presents the activities of Jesus to us as contemporary readers, and we can interpret those activities to determine our practices today. In other words, one need not believe in the inerrancy of Scripture to use this approach. However, the divine inerrancy and preservation of Scripture provide a theological explanation for how texts over two thousand years old accurately describe historical events at that time.

The historical-critical method calls the stability of the text into question. It is important to understand that this method assumes neither that the text has changed nor remained stable. It seeks to investigate that very issue through modern historical methodologies. It also refrains from supernatural explanations of the evolution and preservation of the text.[45]

---

44. "The Chicago Statement on Biblical Inerrancy," 4-6.

45. For more detailed explanations of this method, see Krentz, *The Historical-Critical Method* and Knight, *Methods of Biblical Interpretation*, 19-70.

Thus, this method utilizes several techniques to establish the historical conditions of the text. One of the earliest methods was manuscript analysis. Before the invention of the printing press, scribes copied manuscripts by hand to preserve them. Inevitably, errors entered the manuscripts and could be copied into subsequent manuscripts. Other techniques include archeology, comparative literature, intertextual analysis, and many other tools.

Before discussing this method's presuppositions and limitations, we want to explore another method that is a subcategory of historical criticism: form criticism. Form criticism seeks to understand the genre of the text and the context for its writing.[46] Therefore, the Gospels would have a different form and function than the epistles or Revelation as an apocalyptical work. This method also investigates internal form. Why do the Synoptic Gospels (Matthew, Mark, and Luke) have a different style than John?

Form criticism also investigates the context of the text. This analysis is known as *Sitz im Leben* (life situation). It presumes that every genre of literature has a particular life situation in which it is used. For the Christian scriptures, early uses of form criticism posited that they were used primarily in public worship, particularly in baptisms, early forms of the Eucharist, and preaching. More contemporary scholarship has suggested more possible uses.[47]

In this chapter, form criticism sought to explain the *Sitz im Leben* of the writing and particularly the hearing of Jesus' meal stories at that time. As explained above, the context would have been the early church, very likely in services akin to early forms of the Eucharist, much like today. However, unlike today, Scripture would not have

---

46. For a more detailed explanation of this method, see McKnight, *What is Form Criticism?* and Knight, *Methods of Biblical Interpretation*, 113-126.

47. Knight, *Methods of Biblical Interpretation*, 122.

been widely read at home or for personal devotion, due to the great expense of obtaining manuscripts.

On the surface, this *Sitz im Leben* appears rather commonsensical. We would expect the Scriptures to be read in public worship; after all, Scripture states that very case (Acts 17:2). However, form criticism makes a stronger claim than just that historical probability. It claims that the genre and *Sitz im Leben* influenced the authors or editors in their construction of the text. For example, the editors of the Gospels[48] selected the narratives of Jesus. They placed them in the order found in Scripture not because that is how they happened historically, necessarily, but to accomplish their literary (and theological) aims.

One prominent example is the infancy narratives found in Matthew and Luke. Matthew's infancy narrative includes wise men fleeing to Egypt and Herod's slaughter of the innocents but does not include shepherds. Also, Joseph plays a much more prominent role in Matthew. On the other hand, Luke has shepherds but no wise men, and women, Elizabeth and Mary, play a much more prominent role than Joseph. Scholars using form criticism attribute these differences to Matthew's and Luke's theological aims. Matthew sought to establish Jesus as the King of kings, while Luke sought to establish him as the Savior of the outcasts.

This chapter argued that the meal stories of Jesus cannot be taken at face value. A thorough interpretation of these stories must account for the genre and *Sitz im Leben* in which they were written. Using only a historical-grammatical approach leaves the impression that the editors of the Gospels intended only to tell a historical account of Jesus' ministry. However, a form-critical approach argues that the

---

48. Most contemporary scholars do not believe that the Gospels were written single-handedly by persons named Matthew, Mark, Luke, or John but rather compiled by editors from other sources.

editors intended to make theological claims with the genre used, the inner structure of the Gospels, and accounting for the *Sitz im Leben*, likely a baptized assembly hearing Scripture proclaimed in early Eucharist-like worship services. Thus, these stories have different meanings, as argued above.

Just like the historical-grammatical approach has certain underlying presuppositions, so does the historical-critical approach and its subcategories. Ernst Troeltsch is credited with establishing three principles for this method. First, history only offers a probability of what occurred, not certainty. Historians rely on available data to theorize what may or may not have happened. They cannot claim absolute certainty because new data could radically change such claims.

Second, the "principle of analogy" claims that historical events will likely have occurred similarly to present-day events of like character. For example, if the sun cannot be stopped in the sky by lifting one's arms today, we can presume it could not have been done thousands of years ago (cf. Joshua 10:13).

The final principle is the principle of correlation. This principle implies that all historical phenomena are interrelated. Therefore, a change in one event will cause changes in other events. Using the same example of the stopping of the sun, we know today that the sun does not travel around the Earth but vice versa. We also know that if the Earth were to stop traveling around the sun, which would be the equivalent effect of the sun standing still in the sky, great catastrophes would ensue as gravitational forces would rip the planet apart.

Scholars using a historical-grammatical approach with the presupposition of divine inerrancy would argue that God, as Creator of the Cosmos, could change the laws of nature as desired to allow such miracles to occur as an explanation of the text. Most historical-critical scholars would seek another purpose for the story than just reporting a miracle. That does not presume these scholars believe or disbelieve in miracles, only that they prefer natural explanations for the text to supernatural explanations.

Herein lies the challenge with historical-critical approaches alone. They often leave little room for theological explanations because such explanations presume a divine source. One of the more recent examples of this challenge is the quest for the historical Jesus. Since the Enlightenment, scholars and other prominent people have called into question the supernatural stories in the Bible. One of the most famous examples is Thomas Jefferson's *The Life and Morals of Jesus of Nazareth Extracted Textually from the Gospels in Greek, Latin, French, and English*.[49] Jefferson cut and pasted excerpts from the New Testament of only what he presumed to be Jesus' historical sayings and deeds, omitting most supernatural events. More modern attempts at this work are what has become known as "the quest for the historical Jesus."

Critics of this methodology claim that it goes too far. On the one hand, it has become too historicistic and, therefore, ideological. Rather than simply using historical methods to investigate the text, some historical-critical scholars seek to undermine the theological claims of Christianity through this methodology. While many Christians may feel comfortable questioning the plausibility of Joshua causing the sun to stop moving, the same questions posited toward central tenets of the faith, such as Christ's resurrection and divinity, create significant theological and dogmatic challenges for the Church.

Canonical criticism responded to these concerns.[50] Canonical criticism begins with historical-critical methodologies. It seeks to

---

49. Jefferson, *The Life and Morals of Jesus of Nazareth*.

50. For further explanation of this approach, see Sanders, *Canon and Community* and Knight, *Methods of Biblical Interpretation*, 215-219.

understand the historical conditions of the text, its genre, its *Sitz im Leben*, and the history of its editing.[51] However, it goes further after investigating these various aspects of the text. It seeks to answer the question, "Why did the book's editors (or the canon of Scripture) include this material in this arrangement? What was the theological purpose?" Rather than attempting to sift the wheat of the "purely" historical material from the chaff of the "supernatural" material, canonical criticism recognizes the importance of both types of material in shaping the text.

Therefore, canonical criticism cares less about the author's original intention than the community's theological intention for using the material. Canonical criticism is completely comfortable with intertextual contradictions. For example, canonical criticism would argue that the purpose for the differences in the infancy narratives between Matthew and Luke explains why the Church chose to include both accounts. The Church desired an account that recognizes Christ as the King of kings (Matthew) and one that recognizes him as the Savior of the oppressed (Luke). Both accounts provided important theologies for the Church and were included in the canon.

This chapter utilized canonical criticism in arguing for the traditional Ordo of baptism before communion. Whether or not Jesus performed the miracle of feeding the five thousand or of the four thousand was less important than the theological reason for including the stories. As discussed above, these stories were included to reform the church regarding its eucharistic practice to be more inclusive of the poor and oppressed but not to change the historic Ordo of baptism before communion, which would have undermined the message being proclaimed.

---

51. Known as redaction criticism, one of the subcategories of historical criticism.

Canonical criticism provides a robust hermeneutical tool for the Church. It takes the text seriously, investigating its historical origins with the best scholarship. However, it does not leave the text in tatters, like a Jeffersonian effort of cutting and pasting only the bits we agree with. It respects the entirety of the text. It values theology as a historical tool employed in shaping the canon. Therefore, it takes the theology of the communities involved in the process seriously but does not presume on the reader's theology. One may or may not believe that the sun stood still at Joshua's hand, but one must respect that the community believed this story of enough theological importance to include it in its canon.

As with most theological issues, Scripture speaks with many voices through many communities. Therefore, the Church should be cautious in approaching Scripture for an exact historical account of the practices of the early Church. However, the Church should be equally cautious in disregarding Scripture as an irrelevant source of history. Perhaps the wisest approach might be to recognize that Scripture provides the narrative of various communities' struggles with faith and that these various communities provide the context for the writing of Scripture. Thus, each forms the other and is formed by the other. Proponents of communion without baptism rightly point to the eucharistic character of the narratives of Jesus' table fellowship. However, by not placing them within their narrative and canonical context, they fail to recognize the indissoluble bond between baptism, the Eucharist, and the Church.

CHAPTER TWO

BAPTISM, THE EUCHARIST, AND THE HISTORY OF THE CHURCH

An Indissoluble Bond

In this chapter, we will discuss the indissoluble bond between baptism, the Eucharist, and the Church as perceived through the history of the Church. First, we will show the rich ecclesiological symbolism of baptism and the Eucharist found in the patristic and early medieval periods. Then, we will show how the disintegration of Christian initiation began in the late medieval period and continued during the Continental and English Reformations, correlated with a rise in clericalism. Finally, we will show that the modern attempt to reunify baptism and the Eucharist in The Episcopal Church was meant to strengthen their ecclesiological implications once again.

Baptism and the Eucharist: Rich Ecclesiological Symbols

In the last chapter, we drew attention to the strong connection between baptism, the Eucharist, and the Church in Paul's writings and the Gospels' narrative and canonical contexts. The details of the rites themselves, however, remained unclear. These details gained greater clarity as the Church entered the early second century.

As the Church entered the second and third centuries, it experienced social and political persecution. At times, this persecution became intense, resulting in martyrs for the faith. One of the important symbols that baptism and the Eucharist became was of unity. Preserving the unity of the Church was not just an ideal but an existential necessity. Baptism and the Eucharist acted as agents of unity for the Church amid great persecution.

One of the earliest theologians and martyrs, Justin Martyr (c. 100 CE), wrote in his *First Apology* about the importance of baptism and the Eucharist for the unity of the Church. He gave specific instructions about the admission of the unbaptized into communion. In paragraph one of chapter sixty-five, he described the order of events: first, the candidates were "washed," and then they were led into the eucharistic fellowship.[1] Again, the progression from baptism to the Eucharist is evident. Then, in chapter sixty-six, he stated quite succinctly, "And this food is called by us 'thanksgiving,' of which it is permitted for no one to partake unless he believes our teaching to be true, and has been washed with the washing for forgiveness of sins and regeneration, and so lives as Christ handed down."[2] Like Paul in Galatians, Justin Martyr strongly connected faith and baptism, not faith and the Eucharist. New converts express their faith first in baptism. Then, they can share in the intimacy of the eucharistic meal.

Other patristic authors spoke of the integral relationship between baptism and the Eucharist with vivid imagery. For example, Irenaeus, (c. 202 CE), also a martyr, eloquently wrote,

> For as a compact lump of dough cannot be formed of dry wheat without fluid matter, nor can a loaf possess unity, so,

---

1. Bradshaw, *Eucharistic Origins*, 61.
2. Bradshaw, *Eucharistic Origins*, 61.

in like manner, neither could we, being many, be made one in Christ Jesus without the water from heaven. And as dry earth does not bring forth unless it receives moisture, in like manner we also, being originally a dry tree, could never have brought forth fruit unto life without the voluntary rain from above. For our bodies have received unity among themselves by means of that laver which leads to incorporation; but our souls by means of the Spirit.[3]

Vivid resonances exist between Irenaeus' description and that of Paul in 1 Cor. 10. Like Paul, Irenaeus used this imagery to stress the importance of unity. Baptism did not just prepare the Corinthians for the Eucharist by washing them clean of sin. It also unified them as the collective body of the Church, as water unifies the many grains of wheat into a single lump. Paul also drew a connection between baptism and receiving the Holy Spirit. The waters of baptism incorporated the bodies of the Corinthians into the unity of the Church, and the Holy Spirit incorporated their souls.[4]

In addition to baptism and the Eucharist, the bishop became an important symbol of unity for the Church. As the Church was still growing, the bishop could be the primary officiant at baptisms and the Eucharist, symbolizing the candidates' entry into the Church. The early Church had a unified rite of initiation that involved baptism, anointing (either pre-baptismal, post-baptismal, or both), and then entrance into the eucharistic fellowship, all occurring in a single service by the bishop. These pre-baptismal and post-baptismal anointings had symbolic significance, referring to the anointing of prophets, priests, and kings.

---

3. Irenaeus, "Against the Heresies," 11.

4. We want to be careful about reading this passage anachronistically as body and soul were not understood as separate entities during that time.

For example, the *Didascalia Apostolorum*, which was likely written in northern Syria, states, "[W]ith the imposition of hand you should anoint the head only. As of old priests and kings were anointed in Israel, so do you likewise, with the imposition of hand, anoint the head of those who receive baptism, whether it be of men or of women."[5] Another rite in the *Syrian Acts of the Apostles* also describes a pre-baptismal anointing with detail. Both liturgies emphasize the anointing with oil of the candidate over and above the immersion in water, and both also draw a connection between that anointing and the anointing of kings and priests in the Hebrew Scriptures. This vivid baptismal imagery shows that some people in the early Church connected baptism with priesthood and not just for the remission of sins.[6]

At about the same time in the West, the Gnostic sects were gaining greater popularity. These sects believed that baptism was not necessary for salvation. In fact, faith in Christ was not even necessary. Instead, they taught that *gnosis*, a complex form of esoteric knowledge, was the prerequisite for salvation. In response to this teaching, Tertullian (160-240 CE) wrote the first full Christian treatise on baptism, *De Baptismo*. In this treatise, Tertullian likened baptism to the anointing of Aaron as a high priest by Moses, establishing yet another connection between baptism and priesthood.[7] However, unlike the examples from the Eastern Church above, the order of the rite in Tertullian gives a post-baptismal anointing. He suggests that only after the purification of baptism can the Holy Spirit be received. A person must first die to sin and then be reborn in Christ through the waters of baptism. Only then can they receive the Holy Spirit.

---

5. "Didascalia Apostolorum," 14-15.

6. Bradshaw, *Eucharistic Origins*, 85.

7. Tertullian, "Treatise on Baptism," 36.

Thus, Tertullian provided the first Western theology of baptism based upon Romans 6, in which Paul described baptism as first dying with Christ and then being raised to new life in him.[8]

Cyprian of Carthage (d. 258) was another patristic author who wrote extensively about baptism and the Eucharist. Like Tertullian, he described a post-baptismal anointing. However, he was the first to describe a post-baptismal laying-on of hands by the bishop (possibly consignation) and to use Acts 8 as a theological rationale for this practice.[9] In Acts 8, the apostles encountered a group of Christians who had been baptized in the name of Jesus Christ but had not yet received the Holy Spirit. The apostles laid hands on them, and they received the Holy Spirit. Later, this post-baptismal episcopal action, described by Cyprian, would increase in importance.

While Paul and Irenaeus drew parallels between baptism, the Eucharist, and unity within the Church, Cyprian attempted to make that connection even stronger. He wrote during a great controversy in the Church following the Decian Persecution. The controversy surrounded how to receive those who lapsed from the Church due to persecution back into the communion of the Church.

The Novationists, a sect that formed in Rome, refused to allow those who had lapsed to re-enter communion even after penance. This rigorist stance was too much for the Church. After all, one of the core tenets of Christianity is forgiveness and reconciliation. The Church eventually declared the Novationists to be both heretics and schismatics.

This division in the Church created confusion about Church membership. Cyprian attempted to clarify this confusion by arguing that all heretics and schismatics, Novationist or otherwise, needed

---

8. Johnson, *The Rites of Christian Initiation*, 88.
9. Johnson, *The Rites of Christian Initiation*, 90-92.

to be baptized in the Church. He did not consider it re-baptism because he suggested that baptism in a schismatic group was not truly baptism. Cyprian did not just exhort his followers to greater unity using the imagery of baptism, like Paul and Iarenaeus did. Instead, he completely disconnected baptism and the Eucharist from those who had separated from the Church. While this issue remained unresolved during his lifetime, future church councils did not uphold Cyprian's position.[10]

Cyprian's view of the Eucharist also reflects an increased clericalism. Instead of seeing the entire assembly as anointed priests like Christ, Cyprian taught that the presbyter stands in the place of Christ. In his *Epistles*, he states,

> For if Jesus Christ, our Lord and God, is himself the high priest of God the Father and first offered himself as a sacrifice to the Father, and commanded this to be done in his remembrance, then that priest truly functions in the place of Christ who imitates what Christ did and then offers a true and full sacrifice in the church to God the Father, if he thus proceeds to offer according to what he sees Christ himself to have offered.[11]

Through his teaching, we see a significant theological shift. The focus turned toward the presbyter rather than the full assembly. This shift in focus would intensify with time.

Any discussion of the pre-Nicene liturgical rites of the Church must include *The Apostolic Tradition*. Much debate surrounds the authenticity of this document. Some would attribute it to a bishop of Rome, Hippolytus. However, more recent scholarship has cast doubt

---

10. Johnson, *The Rites of Christian Initiation*, 92-93.
11. Cyprian, "Epistle 63.14," in Bradshaw, *Eucharistic Origins*, 110-111.

upon that attribution.[12] Nonetheless, it still provides a framework for what may have been the ritual practice in Rome just before Nicaea. Most scholars agree that the document does give the general framework for the baptismal rite, which happens to mirror the North African rite closely.

Where it differs, and thus where the controversy begins, is in a second post-baptismal anointing and hand-laying by the bishop. Gregory Dix argued for the authenticity of this section and attributed it to what is now called confirmation. However, Paul Bradshaw and Maxwell Johnson (among other scholars) argue that that section is a later—eleventh to fifteenth-century—addition.[13] This controversy becomes important in later discussions about the role and placement of confirmation in the rites of initiation. Later in this chapter, we will discuss the controversies surrounding confirmation.

As the Church entered the fourth century, a radical shift occurred. In 313 CE, Emperor Constantine signed the Edict of Milan. This edict ended the persecution of the Church, making it legal in the empire and, with his conversion to Christianity, the imperial religion. The Church went from being in the shadows to being fully public. This change also had a profound impact on the Church's worship.

One of the changes that occurred was an increased emphasis on the primary metaphor of baptism as the remission of sins in the West. The baptismal imagery found in Romans 6 (i.e., death and resurrection in Christ) took precedence over other baptismal imageries. The Western Church understood baptism as offering the forgiveness of sins. However, major sins committed after baptism would not be forgiven. Therefore, people would often

---

12. Johnson, *The Rites of Christian Initiation*, 103.
13. Johnson, *The Rites of Christian Initiation*, 96-110.

wait until their deathbed to be baptized out of fear that they might commit an egregious sin that a second baptism could not wash away.[14]

Another liturgical change based on this emphasis of Romans 6 imagery involved the pre-baptismal anointing. It had been associated with the reception of the Holy Spirit but became associated with exorcism to prepare one to die in Christ.[15] Baptism itself was seen as participating in the death, burial, and resurrection of Jesus. The imagery of the baptism of Jesus in the Jordan began to recede as the primary metaphor for baptism itself. In its place, a post-baptismal anointing was added to incorporate the reception of the Holy Spirit, followed by the immediate reception of the Eucharist.[16]

During this time, the connection between baptism and the priesthood persisted. One symbol of this connection was the white raiment, often used today. *The Letter of John the Deacon to Senarius*, written around 500 C.E., provides beautiful imagery of the strong connection between baptism and priesthood:

> He [the baptized person] is next arrayed in white vesture, and his head anointed with the unction of the sacred chrism: that the baptized person may understand that in his person a kingdom and a priestly mystery have met.... For a fuller expression of the idea of priesthood, the head of the neophyte is dressed in a linen array for priests of that time used always

---

14. Johnson, *The Rites of Christian Initiation*, 117.

15. The term "exorcism" can have different meanings. One generally recognized meaning refers to the "binding of spirits" when those spirits inhabit a person or place. Liturgically, however, exorcistic rites entered the baptismal rite of some areas during this time (cf. Johnson, *The Rites of Christian Initiation*, 78-79). Here, I use exorcism in its liturgical sense.

16. Johnson, *The Rites of Christian Initiation*, 155-157.

to deck the head with a certain mystic covering. All the neophytes are arrayed in white vesture to symbolize the resurgent Church. . . . the costume of their second birth should display the raiment of glory so that clad in a wedding garment he may approach the table of the heavenly bridegroom as a new man.[17]

In this imagery, Deacon John connected baptism, priesthood, and the Eucharist. Through baptism, one becomes a priest in God's Church and then is welcomed to the wedding table of the Eucharist.

As late as the sixth century, *Ordo Romanus XI* provided another example of the imagery of priesthood connected with baptismal clothing. This text includes rubrics that quite vividly tie baptism with the priesthood when they instruct the bishop to give the newly baptized a stole, an overgarment, a chrismal cloth, and ten coins. They are then robed, which appears to signify entry into the universal priesthood of the Church.[18]

As mentioned above, the bishop was a primary symbol of church unity and often the officiant for baptisms and the Eucharist in the second and third centuries. However, as the Church grew with its legalization in the fourth century, the bishop could no longer be the primary officiant of baptismal liturgies. Therefore, presbyters took on a more significant role for the bishop. Retaining the significance of the bishop as a symbol of unity was still important. To maintain this symbolism, the Church took two different approaches.

The East preserved the unitive rite of initiation, baptism, anointings, and Eucharist in a single service by having the presbyter

---

17. "John the Deacon," 210-211.
18. Johnson, *The Rites of Christian Initiation*, 228.

chrismate the newly baptized when the bishop could not be present. Using chrism consecrated by the bishop, the connection with the bishop remained symbolically present.[19] This practice remains in effect today in Eastern rite churches.

However, the West took a different approach. The concern for the bishop's personal participation in the rite remained. In a letter from Pope Innocent I to Bishop Decentius of Gubbio, Innocent I stated, "Regarding the signing of infants, this clearly cannot be done validly by anyone other than the Bishop. For even though presbyters are priests, none of them holds the office of pontiff."[20] He then drew a parallel between the laying-on of hands by the apostles of those already baptized as described in Acts and this second post-baptismal anointing and hand-laying. Johnson argues that, considering the historical controversies around *The Apostolic Tradition*, this reference may be the first reference to a second post-baptismal hand-laying reserved only for the bishop. Johnson also argues that the practice of presbyteral anointing and hand-laying was still occurring with some regularity. Otherwise, this letter, and similar letters written by Pope Gelasius I seventy years later and Pope Gregory I one hundred years later, admonishing presbyters not to anoint with chrism consecrated by the bishop or apply "pontifical consignation," would have been unnecessary.[21]

This second hand-laying rite strengthened over time. The Council of Elvira, the First Council of Toledo, the First Council of Arles, and the First Council of Orange all decreed that only a bishop should perform it.[22] It also began being seen as a perfection, completion,

---

19. Johnson, *The Rites of Christian Initiation*, 157.
20. "The Letter of Pope Innocent to Decentius, 416," 206.
21. Johnson, *The Rites of Christian Initiation*, 162–164.
22. Johnson, *The Rites of Christian Initiation*, 180-182.

or *confirmation* of baptism by the bishop. For example, a Pentecost sermon attributed to a fifth-century bishop of Gaul, Faustus of Riez, provides the classic Western definition of confirmation as a strengthening of baptism:

> And because in this world we who will be prevailing must walk in every age between invisible enemies and dangers, we are reborn in baptism for life, and we are confirmed after baptism for the strife. In baptism we are washed; after baptism we are strengthened.[23]

Thus, the theological justification for a separation in the initiatory rite began. However, Johnson points out that the widespread use of this custom of a second hand-laying ceremony at that time is unknown. For example, later Gallican and Mozarabic rites do not include any mention of this second hand-laying ceremony.[24] As with so much of church history, clear linear progressions are less evident than a series of fits and starts, reappraisals, outright refusals in the case of some, and then eventual consistency.

Any discussion of baptism and the Eucharist in the patristic period must involve Augustine of Hippo. Like other theologians before him, Augustine taught the postbaptismal anointing with chrism, signifying the baptizand's new priestly and royal identity and reception of the Holy Spirit.[25] In one of his Easter homilies, Augustine described with beautiful imagery the strong connection between baptism and the Eucharist:

---

23. "Eusebius Gallicanus," 258. Scholars disagree regarding the date and authorship of this sermon. See Dix, *The Theology of Confirmation in Relation to Baptism* and Winkler, "Confirmation or Chrismation," for further details on this debate.

24. Johnson, *The Rites of Christian Initiation*, 185.

25. Johnson, *The Rites of Christian Initiation*, 188.

> Then came the baptism of water; you were moistened, as it were, so as to arrive at the form of bread. But, without fire, bread does not yet exist. What, then, does the fire signify? The chrism. For the sacrament of the Holy Spirit is the oil of our fire... Therefore the fire, that is, the Holy Spirit, comes after the water; then you become bread, that is, the body of Christ. Hence, in a certain manner, unity is signified.[26]

Like Paul, Irenaeus, and Cyprian, Augustine saw the connection between baptism, the Eucharist, and the Church as a complete whole.

Two great controversies in the Western Church led to further refinement of baptismal theology during the fourth century. First was the Donatist controversy. This controversy built on the controversies involving Cyprian in what to do about Christians who betrayed the faith. The Donatists cited Cyprian in suggesting that Christians baptized by priests who had left the Church would need to be rebaptized. They suggested that the sacraments performed by these separated priests were not valid.

Augustine provided a different perspective. He taught that if the proper elements and words were used, the sacrament was valid. The worthiness of the priest was not an issue because Christ is the true minister of all sacraments. From this point forward, this definition of a "valid" sacrament would become the classic definition for the Western Church.[27] Thus, he reversed Cyprian's teaching that the sacraments did not exist outside the Church. However, in doing so, his emphasis on the proper elements and words would lead later to sacramental minimalism.

---

26. Augustine, "Sermon on Easter Morning," 158.
27. Johnson, *The Rites of Christian Initiation*, 189-191.

The next controversy also significantly impacted baptismal theology—the Pelagian controversy. Pelagianism taught that humans are born with free will and thus have the innate capacity to choose good over evil. One of Pelagius' disciples, Celestius, attacked the widespread practice of infant baptism suggesting that it was invalid since an infant is not capable of making a choice yet.

In response to the Pelagians, Augustine developed his theology of "original sin." He taught that human beings are born incapable of making a choice for the good, due not to a lack of cognitive development, but to the effects of sin as passed down from Adam. Augustine used the rites of exorcism that had become an important part of the baptismal rite for both adults and infants as justification for his theology. If the infant participates in the exorcism as does the adult, then the infant must be exorcised of something if the infant has not yet committed a sinful act. Augustine believed that baptism exorcises original sin in the case of the infant.

Thus, Augustine tightened the connection between baptism and the remission of sins and began restricting its theological breadth. Combined with high infant mortality, baptism took on the sole characteristic of preparing infants for eternity should they die suddenly. In this way, Augustine's teaching minimized the dimensions of baptism for the Western Church to a definition of validity and an exorcism of original sin.[28]

However, in the East, this narrowing of baptismal theology did not occur. St. John Chrysostom, in his Sermon to the Neophytes, provided a vivid argument for infant baptism without reference to original sin.

---

28. Johnson, *The Rites of Christian Initiation*, 194-197. Henceforth, the term "exorcism" will be used in reference both to its early liturgical connection to the exorcistic rites themselves and to this development in Augustinian theology regarding the exorcism of original sin.

> Although many men think that the only gift it [baptism] confers is the remission of sins, we have counted its honors to the number of ten. It is on this account that we baptize even infants, although they are sinless, that they may be given the further gifts of sanctification, justice, filial adoption, and inheritance, that they may be brothers and members of Christ, and become dwelling places for the Spirit.[29]

The Church baptizes infants to provide them with the additional benefits of baptism beyond the remission of sins. To this day, Eastern Rite churches teach this more fulsome view of baptism.

The narrowing of baptismal theology and the development of a second post-baptismal hand-laying ceremony in the West would continue to develop in the medieval period. The rich ecclesiological symbolism of baptism and the Eucharist would begin to disappear. Baptism would be seen primarily as an exorcism of original sin without the additional imagery of being anointed as a priest in the Church, resulting in a rise in clericalism.

Disintegration and Disunity: Christian Initiation and the Fracturing of the Church

In the medieval and reformation periods of church history, the unity of the rites of Christian initiation began to disintegrate into separate rites with significant periods of time between them. Baptism became less about initiation into the universal priesthood of the Church and more about exorcism of original sin. The Eucharist took on a realism that separated the laity from active participation. Finally, the rise in clericalism led not only to the centralization of the priest

---

29. John Chrysostom, "Sermon to the Neophytes," 166.

as the consecrator of the elements in the Eucharist but also to the centralization of the pope as the universal monarch of the Church. Eventually, these drastic changes would lead first to the fracturing of the Church between East and West and then to the fracturing of the Church in the West through the Continental and English reformations.

The early medieval period involved fewer differences in the initiatory rites than the patristic period. For example, the Gelasian Sacramentary, one of the earliest extant Roman rites dating back to the eighth century, has the same unitive initiatory rite as existed in the patristic period. It includes a pre-baptismal anointing, baptism, a post-baptismal anointing, the Eucharist, and an episcopal hand-laying rite.[30] Such a later document suggests that this unitive initiatory rite had strong connections within the Church. Only a powerful need could pull it apart.

That need arose in the nearly universal practice of infant baptism by this time. As noted above, Augustine used the practice of infant baptism as the grounds for his theology of original sin. Later, though, a reversal in theology occurred. Augustine's theology of original sin contributed to the promotion of infant baptism. Parents began to have their infants baptized as soon as possible out of fear that they might die while still in sin. This practice is called *quam primum* (as soon as possible) baptism. With this emphasis on *quam primum* baptism, pre-baptismal catechesis began to diminish. Before this time, the parents would come with their infants to pre-baptismal catechesis several times as their own preparation to support their infant later in life. However, with the emphasis on *quam primum* baptism and the fear that the theology of original sin evoked, catechesis was reduced to a single, very simplified rite at the church door right before the baptismal rite.[31]

---

30. Fisher, *Christian Initiation: Baptism in the Medieval West*, 17-19.
31. Johnson, *The Rites of Christian Initiation*, 258-260.

Eventually, the desire for *quam primum* baptisms became so urgent that priests would visit the home near the birth or midwives would perform emergency baptisms immediately after birth. Thus, baptism moved from occurring in the church to the home. Rather than being an ecclesial affair, welcoming one into the Body of Christ, it became a private, familial affair out of necessity.

In the eighth century, Charlemagne, as Holy Roman Emperor, began to centralize authority both civically and ecclesiastically. In his desire to unify his empire, he requested liturgical rites from Pope Hadrian in Rome. Before Charlemagne, a diversity of rites had existed in the Franco-Germanic lands. However, the Roman rites were papal liturgies and not well-suited for the average country parish. The liturgies needed to be adapted for this new environment.

One of these liturgical adaptations involved baptism. Alcuin, bishop for Charlemagne in Gaul, described an initiatory rite consisting of baptism, chrismation, communion, and episcopal hand-laying. Alcuin's disciple, Rabbanus Maurs, archbishop of Mayence and a disciple of Alcuin, later described the initiatory rite as above but spoke of the episcopal hand-laying rite occurring seven days after baptism. This marks the first record of an interval between baptism and confirmation, which would eventually grow longer.

Fisher argues that the prevailing practice during this time remained presbyteral baptism, chrismation, and communion with no later episcopal acts. However, as Charlemagne began to enforce the use of the Roman rite exclusively, a second episcopal hand-laying rite was added to the initiatory rite to accommodate the papal liturgy. Only later will the theological justifications for this second, separate rite come to provide the explanation for what began as an imperial decree. Thus, the initiatory rite began to disintegrate.[32]

Along with the changes in the initiatory rite came changes in eucharistic theology. In the ninth century, a monk, Paschasius Radbertus, published a treatise on eucharistic theology. He focused on the connection between the sacramental Body of Christ and the historical Body of Christ by stressing a somatic real presence. With this emphasis on eucharistic realism, he flattened the multidimensional aspects of the Eucharist into a purely "thingly" concept.[33] The Eucharist no longer contained the rich ecclesiological imagery seen in Paul, Irenaeus, Cyprian, and Augustine. Now, it became the actual flesh of Christ.

By the eleventh and twelfth centuries, great changes occurred in the Church. Pope Gregory VII completely reorganized the Church under a more centralized authority. He attributed unprecedented powers to the papacy and drew around him assistant clergy who would eventually become the powerful Roman Curia in whose hands would be the election of new popes. During this same period, the Church experienced the first Great Schism between the East and the West. While precursors to this schism existed centuries earlier, 1054 C.E. marked the official split between Constantinople and Rome.[34]

Also, in the eleventh century, eucharistic theology developed further in this "thingly" direction with the Berengarian controversy. Initially, Berengar emphasized the spiritual dimensions of the Eucharist over an ever-growing eucharistic realism. However, his spiritual emphasis on the Eucharist would get him called before Rome on heresy charges. In his denouncement of his earlier teachings,

---

32. Fisher, *Christian Initiation: Baptism in the Medieval West*, 67.
33. Kilmartin, *The Eucharist in the West*, 83–84.
34. MacCulloch, *The Reformation*, 26.

he signed a document in which he stated that the eucharistic elements are transformed "substantially." This statement became the precursor to the doctrine of transubstantiation.[35]

This emphasis on eucharistic realism also impacted the rites of initiation as questions began to arise about infant communion. Some people argued that if the elements were the actual Body and Blood of Christ, then they should not be given to infants who might not fully consume them. In response to these concerns, scholastic theologians such as William of Champeaux and Radulphus Ardens began to promote the distribution of only wine for infants.[36] The infant who was once anointed as a priest and clothed in a stole could no longer fully partake in the Eucharist. Eventually, the Church restricted the cup to only the celebrant. No communicants, infants or adults, could partake of the cup. This restriction further disintegrated the baptismal-eucharistic bond that had once united the congregation in the Eucharist.

As the status of the eucharistic elements grew due to a greater focus on eucharistic realism, the Church placed more emphasis on proper preparation to receive Holy Communion. Ecclesial officials argued that only those duly prepared should receive such a great mystery. This emphasis on proper preparation led to a drastic decline in lay communication. Eventually, the Fourth Lateran Council responded to this decline in communion by declaring that each person must receive it at least once a year after reaching the "age of reason." This requirement becomes known as "the Easter duty." Later interpretations of this declaration then limited communion to only after the "age of reason."[37]

---

35. Kilmartin, *The Eucharist in the West*, 98-100.
36. Fisher, *Christian Initiation: Baptism in the Medieval West*, 102.
37. Fisher, *Christian Initiation: Baptism in the Medieval West*, 103.

The constellation of all these various changes eventually led to the tearing apart of the unitive initiatory rite into separate rites. The complete rite of initiation for both adults and infants as priests into the Church had become simply infant baptism. It became a type of operation to be completed on the infant with the sole purpose of exorcising original sin. Out of fear that their infants might die suddenly, parents asked their presbyters, or sometimes even their midwives, to baptize their children in their homes rather than in the Church, morphing baptism into primarily a private rite in the home rather than a public rite for all of the Church to witness.[38] Thus, baptism became a private rite of exorcism for the individual rather than a corporate rite of initiation into the universal priesthood of the Church.

Along with these changes in the theology of baptism and the Eucharist, the theology of ordination also changed significantly. With the emphasis on eucharistic realism, the power to affect this change in the elements became centralized in the hands of the presbyter. By the end of the first millennium, the presbyter alone had the power of consecration. Now, through ordination, the priest gained from Christ the power to transubstantiate the elements into the real Body and Blood of Christ.[39] Baptism was no longer seen as ordination into the universal priesthood but as an exorcistic rite. The Eucharist became an act done by the priest on behalf of the people rather than the full celebration of the people, the Body of Christ. The ecclesiological implications of these radical changes in baptism and the Eucharist would become even more evident in the Reformation period.

The sixteenth century brought another radical change to the Western Church. Martin Luther's posting of his Ninety-Five Theses

---

38. Johnson, *The Rites of Christian Initiation*, 265.
39. Kilmartin, *The Eucharist in the West*, 129-132.

to his bishop in Wittenberg marked the beginning of this period. Rather than *the* Reformation, this period is better identified as the Continental and English reformations, as England alone had four. While these reformations impacted all aspects of the Church, they had a particular focus on its worship.

Eucharistic realism and papal primacy became two key issues around which the reformers debated. Nicholas Ridley, bishop of London (d. 1555) emphasized the importance of these two factors,

> [M]ethink I perceive two things to be [Satan's] most perious and most dangerous engines which he hath to impugn Christ's verity, his Gospel, his faith: and the same two also to be the most massy posts and most mighty pillars, whereby he maintaineth and upholdeth his Satanical synagogue. These two, sir, are they in my judgment: the one his false doctrine and idolatrical use of the Lord's supper; and the other, the wicked and abominable usurpation of the primacy of the see of Rome.[40]

As discussed above, baptism had faded into the background as a mostly private rite to be performed as soon as possible after birth to exorcise original sin before any threat of sudden death. While the reformers agreed that baptism was one of the dominical rites of the Church, the primary focus of their debates concerned the doctrines of transubstantiation and the primacy of the Pope of Rome. Due to this project's scope, our focus will primarily be on Christian initiation in the Church of England.

During the reign of King Henry VIII, the Church of England continued to use the Latin Sarum rite, which was prevalent in England at this time, even after the break with Rome. Commentaries on this

---

40. Christmas, ed., *The Works of Nicholas Ridley*, 366.

rite speak little about the ecclesiological implications of baptism. For example, *The Bishop's Book* only emphasized the soteriological aspect of baptism as washing away original sin. *The King's Book*, which was published in 1543, also took a conservative view of baptism. However, it briefly spoke of baptism ecclesiologically: it stated that no person could be a member of the Church except through baptism. Another liturgical commentary, *The Rationale of Ceremonial*, on the other hand, does pick up the multivalent symbolism of baptism with the familiar images of the anointing of kings, priests, and prophets.[41] Thus, this royal priestly imagery surrounding baptism had not completely faded from the memory of the Church in England.

In 1547, King Henry VIII died, making his son Edward VI king at the age of nine. Many bishops, priests, and scholars sought to further the reforms in the Church of England. Thomas Cranmer, the Archbishop of Canterbury, was among them. In 1549, Parliament promulgated the first BCP for the Church of England, of which Cranmer is believed to have been the chief architect.

This prayer book furthers the separation of the initiatory rites that had occurred during the medieval period by developing two rites for baptism: a public rite and a private rite. The public rite appears to hold preference as it occurs first in the ordering of the book. Additionally, the rubrics prescribe the private rite to be used only when the parents are unable to bring their child to the church. Nonetheless, the practice of *quam primum* baptism continued as the rubrics in the private rite indicate

The pastours and curates shall oft admonyshe the people, that they differ [defer] not the Baptisme of infantes any longer then the

---

41. Fisher, *Christian Initiation: Baptism in the Medieval West*, 72-84.

> *Sondaye, or other holy daye, nexte after the chylde bee borne, onlesse upon a great and reasonable cause declared to the curate and by hym approved.*[42]

Due to the difficulties of traveling so soon after childbirth, most parents opted for the private rite of baptism to be conducted in their home rather than the public rite in the church. So even though the public rite had preference by virtue of its order and rubrical instruction, the private rite took precedence in actual practice due to the influence of *quam primum* baptism.

Along with the practical realities of *quam primum* baptism, the primary baptismal theology of the 1549 BCP also centered on the exorcism of original sin. The public rite of baptism contains seven different instances of exorcistic theology: the very first exhortation, the opening prayer, the pre-baptismal consignation, an actual exorcism itself, the prayer before the interrogations, the vesting in the white garment, and the post-baptismal unction with chrism. In contrast, it contains only two instances of ecclesiological language: the opening exhortation and the opening prayer. Even rich ecclesiological symbols like the vesting in the white garment become exorcistic when it says,

> TAKE this white vesture for a token of the innocencie, whiche by Gods grace in this holy sacramente of Baptisme, is given unto thee: and for a signe wherby thou art admonished, so long as thou lyvest, to geve thyselfe to innocencie of living, that, after this transitorye lyfe, thou mayest be partaker of the lyfe everlasting. Amen.[43]

---

42. 1549BCP, 52–53.
43. 1549BCP, 51.

Instead of a symbol of royal priestly initiation, the white garment was now a symbol of purity and innocence from original sin.

This preoccupation with sin was also evident in the communion rite. The rite begins with two paragraphs of rubrics emphasizing that those wishing to communicate should not be notorious sinners and should be reconciled with their fellow Christians before coming to communion. The rite then continues with two long exhortations about receiving communion worthily. Finally, the general confession comes immediately after the Eucharistic Prayer just before communion.[44] This placement of the general confession immediately before the reception of communion again indicates the need to receive worthily as it minimizes the time between absolution and reception to the least degree possible. Furthermore, no ecclesiological references exist in the communion rite except in the Nicene Creed.

The 1549 BCP also emphasized the need for a considerable period between baptism and confirmation to be used for preparation. The exhortation to the godparents at the end of the public and private baptismal rites directs that the newly baptized are to be instructed in the Creed, the Lord's Prayer, and the Ten Commandments.[45] Then, the confirmation rite not only reiterates that the confirmands should be able to recite these three church articles but also instructs them to answer the catechism. For emphasis, the catechism was placed immediately before the confirmation rite.

This concern for proper instructional preparation extended to communion through the "confirmation rubric" at the end of the rite. It says, "*And there shal none be admitted to the holye communion: untill suche time as he be confirmed.*"[46] This rubric encoded one of the reformation

---

44. 1549BCP, 32-33.
45. 1549BCP, 52.
46. 1549BCP, 63.

principles that one must be prepared for communion not only through the purification of baptism but also through catechetical instruction. Catechesis shifted from being pre-baptismal to pre-confirmation. This rubric reinforced the separation of baptism, confirmation, and communion.

The 1549 BCP was not reformed enough for many, so Parliament promulgated a new revision only three years later, which Cranmer also compiled. Martin Bucer, who fled from Strasbourg to England in 1549, wrote a commentary on the 1549 BCP at the behest of Thomas Cranmer called *Bucer's Censura*. In this commentary, he advised removing the giving of the white garment to the baptizand and using chrism because people would not understand their significance.[47] Thus, the new revision utterly vanquished these rich ecclesiological symbols from the rite. However, it also reduced the amount of exorcistic theology by removing the exorcism and by moving the general confession from after the Eucharistic Prayer to before the Eucharistic Prayer.[48] Even with these changes, though, the 1552 BCP still contains a preponderance of exorcistic theology.

Over a century later, with the Restoration, the 1662 BCP became the official edition of the prayer book for the Church of England and remains so today. The exorcistic theology in the baptismal rite and the exhortations for worthy reception in the eucharistic rite of the 1552 BCP remain in the 1662 BCP. However, one important change occurred with the "confirmation rubric." This edition changes the rubric to "*And there shall none be admitted to the holy Communion, until such time as he be confirmed, or be ready and desirous to be confirmed.*"[49] The

---

47. Fisher, *Christian Initiation: The Reformation Period*, 100.

48. 1559BCP, 142 and 133-134, respectively. The texts of the 1552 and 1559 BCPs are identical in this regard.

49. 1662BCP, 433.

phrase "or be ready and desirous to be confirmed" was an important addition due to the trouble preceding the end of the English Civil War and the Act of Uniformity. Since the Commonwealth had abolished the episcopate, no bishops could perform confirmations. With the restoration of the episcopacy, this permissive rubric allowed much of the Church to remain members in good standing since they were "ready and desirous to be confirmed." This rubric would also have important implications for the future Protestant Episcopal Church in the United States, as we will show later in this chapter.

From its height as a unitive symbol of royal priestly initiation into the Church, Christian initiation had now disintegrated into separate rites. The emphasis in baptism was upon exorcism of original sin rather than initiation into the Church. Eucharistic realism and its close counterpart, clericalism, rose to a fever pitch in the High Middle Ages, only to result in the fracturing of the Western Church in the reformations. While a great deal of attention was paid to disputing eucharistic realism and clericalism, little change occurred in the exorcistic baptismal theology of the Church of England. The connection between baptism, the Eucharist, and the Church would not begin to reunify until the contemporary era.

A Brief Excursus on the Founding of The Episcopal Church in the United States

The history of the founding of The Episcopal Church is rich and complex.[50] For the purposes of this project, we will highlight one key development in the early history of The Episcopal Church that

---

50. For an excellent survey of this history, see Prichard, *A History of the Episcopal Church*.

laid an important foundation for more substantial changes to occur later—the use of patristic sources in the first American BCP. The liturgical reformers in the twentieth century would use this patristic rapprochement begun in the early history of the Church much more robustly.

In 1789, the General Convention of the newly formed Protestant Episcopal Church in the United States of America adopted its first BCP. This prayer book included an important change in eucharistic theology from its predecessor the 1662 English BCP. Samuel Seabury, the first person consecrated as a bishop in this fledgling church, would influence this change.

Due to the tensions between the newly burgeoning United States of America and its former motherland England, Seabury needed to travel to the Scottish Episcopal Church rather than the Church of England for his consecration as bishop. While in Aberdeen, Scotland, Seabury received an introduction from John Johnson of Cranbrook to a eucharistic theology distinct from that used in the Church of England based on Johnson's study of patristic sources. Johnson became convinced that the 1662 Communion Office was deficient. It only used the Institution Narrative and did not include an oblation or epiclesis, an invocation of the Holy Spirit. By including the epiclesis, "And we most humbly beseech thee, O merciful Father, to hear us, and of thy almighty goodness vouchsafe to bless and sanctify, with thy word and holy Spirit, these thy gifts and creatures of bread and wine, that they may become the body and blood of thy most dearly beloved Son," he believed the prayer to be more complete. Seabury agreed with this theology and attempted to promulgate it in his home diocese of Connecticut. However, when Provost William Smith became aware of the Scots Prayer of Consecration, as it was called, he wrote to William White and Samuel Parker decrying this prayer as favoring the doctrine of transubstantiation.[51]

Recognizing that he might face difficulties in convincing the General Convention of The Episcopal Church to adopt these changes, Seabury wrote to William White, now also consecrated a bishop in The Episcopal Church, on June 29, 1789, laying out his defense for these changes. His argument persuaded the General Convention to adopt the Scottish Communion Office with only one slight alteration. The Scottish Communion Office asked that the elements might "become the body and blood of thy most dearly beloved Son." However, the 1789 General Convention instituted the phrase, "that we, receiving them [the consecrated elements] according to thy Son our Saviour Jesus Christ's holy Institution, in remembrance of his Death and Passion, may be partakers of his most blessed Body and Blood." Thus, they retained the structure of the Scottish Communion Office with the institution narrative, oblation, and epiclesis but eliminated the phrasing that raised the concern of transubstantiation.[52]

Thus, with this diversion from the 1662 BCP, the composers of the American BCP began an important journey back to patristic sources that would eventually lead to the reunification of the initiatory rites in the twentieth century. The next prayer book revision in 1892 did not include any major alterations from 1789.[53] However, the 1928 BCP was the most significant revision up to that time. Then, the 1979 BCP introduced an entirely new theological point of view. All these changes drew upon patristic sources for their justification.

---

51. Steiner, *Samuel Seabury*, 346-348.
52. Steiner, *Samuel Seabury*, 351-354.
53. Chorley, "The New American Prayer Book: Its History and Contents."

An Attempt to Reunify: Ecumenism and Christian Initiation in The Episcopal Church

As The Episcopal Church entered the twentieth century, many new changes occurred. Two great movements in the wider church had a profound impact on The Episcopal Church and its view of initiation: the ecumenical movement and the liturgical movement. Both movements overlapped, interplayed, and strengthened each other. While we will consider them separately, we do not wish to suggest that they were working in isolation.

The ecumenical movement was well underway by the late nineteenth and early twentieth centuries, as cooperation both within denominations (the first Anglican Lambeth Conference in 1867, for example) and among denominations increased. However, the Edinburgh Missionary Conference in 1910 marked the birth of the modern ecumenical movement. From this conference, two groups, the "Life and Work" group and the "Faith and Order" group, attempted to unify their ecumenical efforts. However, the world wars put a stop to that effort by hindering most attempts at dialogue. Finally, after two world wars, the World Council of Churches (WCC) convened in 1948, joining the many Protestant denominations, and eventually including Eastern and Oriental Orthodox churches. The Roman Catholic Church chose not to join (and still today chooses only to participate in) the WCC.[54]

The rise of the ecumenical movement affected The Episcopal Church's liturgical life primarily through the issue of admission to communion. With the "confirmation rubric" still in place, only confirmed persons in The Episcopal Church could receive communion. Thus, faithful members of other Protestant denominations, the

---

54. Mullin, *A Short World History of Christianity*, 245-252.

Roman Catholic Church, and Orthodox Churches, while baptized, could not receive communion in The Episcopal Church (except in emergencies). Similarly, Anglicans/Episcopalians could only receive communion in an Anglican/Episcopal Church. The 1930 Lambeth Conference set down a general principle that Anglicans could receive from another church if an Anglican church was not available, and similarly, members of other Christian churches could receive communion in an Anglican church if their church was not available.[55]

However, events would soon challenge this restriction. At a World Conference on Christian Life and Work (a precursor to the WCC) in 1937, Archbishop of Canterbury Cosmo Gordon Lang celebrated the Eucharist and invited all baptized Christians to receive. This public act opened debate in the Anglican Communion about intercommunion. Then the Episcopal Evangelical Fellowship argued that confirmation in The Episcopal Church (or another member church of the Anglican Communion) was not necessary to receive communion in The Episcopal Church. They asserted that since baptism and the Eucharist were the only two sacraments officially recognized by The Episcopal Church, the Church should not consider confirmation a prerequisite to communion. The debate heightened in the 1950s as Angus Dun, the bishop of Washington, invited all Christian ministers attending a conference to receive communion. Then President Eisenhower, a Presbyterian, publicly received communion at an Episcopal Church, thereby furthering the debate. Finally, at the General Convention of 1967, the House of Bishops passed a resolution allowing intercommunion for all baptized Christians. However, the House of Deputies deferred the

---

55. Meyers, "The renewal of Christian initiation in the Episcopal Church, 1928-1979," 104.

resolution to a committee.⁵⁶ The issue would have to be resolved later.

In addition to the ecumenical movement, the liturgical movement had a profound effect on the liturgy of The Episcopal Church. The liturgical movement desired to revitalize the Church's life through a renewed understanding of the role of liturgy in its common life. The leaders of this movement saw a vital link between life and liturgy. Worship must address contemporary life.⁵⁷

In 1946, this desire for liturgical renewal took on organizational reality within The Episcopal Church through the establishment of the Associated Parishes, whose mission was (and still is) to renew the liturgical life of The Episcopal Church. One of the central aims of the liturgical renewal movement, and the Associated Parishes in particular, was to reconsider the role of baptism. As discussed above, most of the Church at that time considered baptism a private affair between the family and the priest. However, as patristic scholarship around the early roots of baptism increased, the links between baptism and the life of the Church also increased. Thus, calls for public baptism abounded, as exemplified in articles in *The Living Church* and public statements made by bishops to their congregations. By the 1960s, the Church began to see baptism less as an exorcism of original sin and more as a sacrament of ministry.

As early as 1943, the Standing Liturgical Commission (SLC) of The Episcopal Church requested at the General Convention that the process of prayer book revision begin.⁵⁸ Due to internal controversies,

---

56. Meyers, "The renewal of Christian initiation in the Episcopal Church, 1928-1979," 106-113.

57. Meyers, "The renewal of Christian initiation in the Episcopal Church, 1928-1979," 49.

58. Initially, the House of Bishops soundly rejected the motion for prayer book revision. After receiving this rejection, the SLC discussed a new approach to prayer

the SLC published *Prayer Book Studies (PBS) I* in 1950 to discuss prayer book revision.[59] *PBS I* outlines the history of the rites of initiation in the Western Church. This early phase of prayer book revision still emphasized the separation of baptism and confirmation. However, it made an important statement on baptismal theology.

> It would certainly be an intolerable doctrine which denied that by Baptism in Water in the Name of all three Persons of the Holy Trinity the Holy Spirit was not given to the baptized, or that He acted upon the baptized purely in an external way. One cannot become a member of Christ or of His Church, which is His Body, and not be a partaker of His Spirit.[60]

Thus, *PBS I* began to revitalize the connection of baptism with membership in the Church rather than simply exorcism of original sin.

In 1962, the SLC proposed a unified initiatory rite for the first time. Recognizing that the rest of The Episcopal Church may not accept a unified rite, they suggested using the word "strengthen" rather than "send" for the Holy Spirit in the confirmation rite. Thus, God sends the Holy Spirit in baptism rather than in confirmation. While this was a small step, it was important in reunifying the initiatory rites.

---

book revision. Past prayer book revisions occurred through an appointed committee procedure that would then develop the proposed prayer book to be approved by General Convention. At the SLC's meeting in 1946, Earl Maddux discussed the process of prayer book revision used in South Africa as an alternative process. This process involved a series of prayer book studies for trial use. The SLC approved this process and sought funding from the next General Convention, "The renewal of Christian initiation in the Episcopal Church, 1928-1979," 62-72.

59. Meyers, "The renewal of Christian initiation in the Episcopal Church, 1928-1979," 149-151.

60. *Prayer Book Studies I: Baptism and Confirmation*, 21.

Then, in 1964, the SLC formed a Drafting Committee to begin laying out the rite. Initially, they called the rite "Holy Baptism with the laying-on-of-hands," which reunified baptism and confirmation into one rite. However, initially, the Drafting Committee did not address a major problem with the reunification of baptism and confirmation. Many in The Episcopal Church considered confirmation as the way in which those coming from communions without apostolic succession could receive the laying-on of hands and become members of The Episcopal Church. They wondered how those coming from other communions without apostolic succession would enter The Episcopal Church if the baptismal and confirmation rites were reunified. Nonetheless, the Drafting Committee remained steadfast not to have a separate rite for that purpose. Instead, they chose to include a rubric that anyone joining The Episcopal Church from another communion could present themselves to the officiant at a public service of baptism to receive the laying-on of hands.[61]

However, this proposal produced controversy, particularly surrounding the role of the bishop. The Drafting Committee's initial proposal suggested that the bishop be the normal and regular officiant for baptism, with the priest acting on behalf of the bishop only when necessary. However, since bishops would likely not officiate at all baptisms in their dioceses, priests would be the *de facto* officiants. This change would mean that the priest could perform the entire initiatory rite without the bishop's being involved. Many people in The Episcopal Church, particularly bishops, raised concerns about this significant change.[62]

---

61. Meyers, "The renewal of Christian initiation in the Episcopal Church, 1928-1979," 180-227.

62. Meyers, "The renewal of Christian initiation in the Episcopal Church, 1928-1979," 228-230.

To respond to this controversy, the Drafting Committee solicited greater involvement. They sought more input regarding this proposed rite of baptism than any other rites considered in the entire prayer book revision. They published PBS 18, which spoke solely to these proposed changes. PBS 18 strongly advocated a unified initiatory rite that reintegrated baptism, confirmation, and communion.

> The basic principle of this proposal is the reunion of Baptism, Confirmation, and Communion into a single continuous service, as it was in the primitive Church. Thus, the entire service will be recognized as the full reception of the candidate into the family of God by the power of the Holy Spirit: Beginning with the acceptance, through faith, of forgiveness of sins and redemption in Christ—of burial with Christ in water in order that we may rise in him to newness of life; followed by the conferring of the gifts of the Spirit by the Laying-on-of-hands; and ending with participation in the holy meal at which the entire family is united, nourished, and sanctified.[63]

It continued by directly linking this unified initiatory rite with the priesthood of all believers. It also suggested that the separation of confirmation into a different rite had caused confusion and emphasized joining a denomination (i.e., The Episcopal Church) rather than initiation into the mystical Body of Christ, the Church. Furthermore, *PBS 18* stressed that "the use of Chrism provides a vivid reminder that Baptism is the ordination of the laity into the servant ministry of the Lord—a birth into the covenanted community which serves the world in the name of Christ."[64] Thus,

---

63. *Prayer Book Studies 18: On Baptism and Confirmation*, 19.
64. *Prayer Book Studies 18: On Baptism and Confirmation*, 23.

PBS 18 emphasized a unified rite and reintroduced the ecclesiological symbolism and theology present in the early rites before the medieval and reformation periods.

Not everyone responded positively to this change. The Drafting Committee received numerous responses asking for some rite in which one could make a public, mature commitment of faith. In response to those requests, the committee drafted a "Form of Commitment to Christian Service." However, it was not broadly utilized. People raised concerns about using this rite in trial use: What exactly is a person's status in The Episcopal Church with this rite? Will people, particularly children, be admitted to communion in some parishes but not in others? In response, the SLC sent out a questionnaire to all the bishops. Seventy-five percent responded. The large majority continued to hold concerns about delegating confirmation to a priest. Nonetheless, at the General Convention in 1970, the House of Bishops (with the House of Deputies concurring) approved *PBS 18* for trial use.

Due in large part to these varied responses, the SLC chose to publish *PBS 26* on Holy Baptism. The Drafting Committee made major amendments to the rite, which were then scrutinized by the SLC. The House of Bishops convened a special meeting to specifically address Christian initiation. It met in Dallas, Texas, from December 6-9, 1972. They issued a "Statement of Agreed Position." In this statement, they said, "There is one, and only one, unrepeatable act of Christian initiation, which makes a person a member of the Body of Christ."[65] They further reiterated in this agreed position that "Christian initiation is normatively administered in a liturgical rite that also includes the laying-on of hands, consignation (with or without Chrism), prayer for the gift of the Holy Spirit, reception

---

65. *Prayer Book Studies 26: Holy Baptism*, 3.

by the Christian community, joining the eucharistic fellowship, and commissioning for Christian mission."[66] After receiving responses, the Drafting Committee made changes to *PBS 26*. Finally, the Presiding Bishop and the President of the House of Deputies approved it for trial use in the church.[67]

The new prayer book was almost ready to be approved. However, before final approval, some important changes still needed to be made. The Committee on the Contents and Order of the Draft Proposed Book suggested that Baptism be removed from the Pastoral Offices section and placed before the Eucharist section. This change in position in the prayer book indicated that baptism was no longer one of several pastoral offices intended to meet the needs of individuals. Instead, it was now a primary rite of The Episcopal Church.[68] Finally, the SLC completed the Draft Proposed Book of Common Prayer, which the General Convention of 1976 approved for use. Then, the General Convention of 1979 approved the final draft and current BCP.[69]

Even after this monumental achievement, the work of reunifying the initiatory rites continued. While confirmation remained a separate rite in the 1979 BCP, the revisers of the prayer book, the House of Bishops, and others involved in approving this major revision all agreed that baptism is full initiation in the Church. No other rite is necessary. Nonetheless, questions about how The Episcopal Church could provide an opportunity for a public, mature affirmation of faith that involved the bishop, but would not be confused with a second initiatory rite, continued.

---

66. *Prayer Book Studies 26: Holy Baptism*, 4.

67. Meyers, "The renewal of Christian initiation in the Episcopal Church, 1928-1979," 301-305.

68. Please see chapter three for more development of this contention.

69. Meyers, "The renewal of Christian initiation in the Episcopal Church, 1928-1979," 315-316.

A strong ecclesiological impulse underlay this work of reunification. Much of the exorcistic language had been removed from the baptismal rite, with the ecclesiological symbolism of consignation and optional chrismation returning. However, the disintegration of the initiatory rites took centuries to accomplish. Even though the official rites of The Episcopal Church have changed, it will take much time for the theology of a reunified initiatory rite to be received throughout the church.

Diving Deeper

Why study the history of liturgical rites? Answers to this question vary. Some might suggest we study liturgical history to discover when the rites were "pure" and return to that pristine state. The "early church" often fills that role. Many people, both historically and currently, have believed that a return to the "early church" would right the wrongs that [fill in the blank] created. For the reformers, the pope and the medieval system were the perpetrators. Currently, Constantine and his imperialism have been a focus. This temptation to find the ones responsible and reverse their mistakes is strong.

The challenge with this approach is that no pristine historical period ever existed for the Church. From its inception, it has struggled to be faithful and has often been found wanting. The Church in the apostolic, Nicene, medieval, and reformation periods had challenges. Liturgical history assists in uncovering those challenges and how the Church tried to meet them through its worship practices.

Others study liturgical history not to recover a pristine past but to justify current practice. This endeavor often takes the shape of direct lineage. They begin with today and attempt to draw a straight line through history to their preconceived origin, in the case of the Church, Christ. Since the Church considers Scripture authoritative, this approach appears justified by attempting to validate current practice scripturally.

However, this attempt to create a direct lineage to Scripture makes two faulty assumptions. First, it assumes that the point of origin is historically consistent and that Scripture's purpose is to convey that consistent historical account. As chapter one elucidates, Scripture was never meant to be read as a history book. Historical criticism has raised many questions about the historicity of Scripture. Scripture's purpose is to convey the theological convictions of diverse communities.

Second, it assumes that history permits linear progressions from an origin to today. As recently as the mid-twentieth century, scholars believed that liturgical rites had a uniform shape that could be traced back to the early church.[70] However, more recent scholarship critiques this view in favor of greater liturgical diversity.[71] Our own study in this chapter revealed an abundance of practices related to baptism, confirmation, and the Eucharist. Liturgical history and other historical disciplines quickly dispel the myth of any direct lineage.

Finally, another approach is to abandon history altogether. Those who take this approach have varied reasons. Some find liturgical history too complex and despair over it. If liturgical history is this complicated, how can we use it for today's decisions? They take liturgical history seriously but do not see a path forward. They desire some way to discern through the seemingly overwhelming volume of data.

Others recognize the failures of the Church's past and seek a new path forward. The Holy Spirit is doing a new thing! Liturgical history

---

70. For the most prominent proponent of a uniform shape, see Dix, *The Shape of the Liturgy*.

71. For critiques of Dix's work, see Bradshaw, *The Search for the Origins of Christian Worship* and Spinks, "Mis-Shapen: Gregory Dix and the Four-Action Shape of the Liturgy."

is important only in how it reveals the need for reform. While the Church has certainly made its mistakes, its history is not all bad or all good. This view of liturgical history lacks nuance in its desire to abandon history altogether.

What, then, is the purpose of liturgical history? Each of these approaches—reclaiming the past, finding a lineage through the past, or abandoning the past—has the same focus: the past. But is not history about the past? The eminent liturgical scholar Robert Taft offers an alternative and insightful perspective.

> Liturgical history, therefore, does not deal with the past, but with tradition, which is a *genetic vision of the present*, a present conditioned by its understanding of its roots. And the purpose of this history is not to recover the past (which is impossible), much less to imitate it (which would be fatuous), but to *understand liturgy* which, because it has a history, can only be understood in motion, just as the only way to understand a top is to spin it.[72]

Taft offers a dynamic view of liturgical history in this metaphor of a spinning top. Liturgical history is not a static object to be studied. It is ever-evolving. Attempting to capture a historical moment and preserve it in amber fails to recognize this constant energy.

Instead of connecting liturgical history with the past, Taft connects it with tradition. Here, he claims the view that tradition is living. His reference to it as "a genetic vision of the present" evokes this living imagery. Genetics plays an important role in living things. However, just as genes alone do not determine an organism's present being, tradition alone does not determine the Church's present being.

---

72. Taft, "The Structural Analysis of Liturgical Units: An Essay in Methodology, 317-318.

Scientists today speak of mapping the genome in their attempt to better understand human genetics. Similarly, liturgical history can provide a map. How do we read this map of liturgical history? Some have attempted to read it through understanding the meaning of the rites. Medieval theologians often allegorized aspects of the liturgy, giving each element a mystical meaning. For example, the altar was not just the location on which the elements were placed but the tomb of Christ. The water poured into the wine symbolized the blood and water poured out from Christ's side on the cross.

The challenge with this allegorical approach is that meanings change. New interpretations occur and become popular. Older interpretations die out. Also, symbols, by their nature, are multivalent, having many meanings. The mixed chalice mentioned above has meant many things including the blood and water poured out from Christ's side, his divinity and humanity, the divinity of Christ and the humanity of the Church, and more.[73]

Therefore, Taft argues that meaning cannot be the map of liturgical history. Meaning is too susceptible to subjectivity, which changes as the subjects change. Instead, Taft argues for structure as the map.

> For in the history of liturgical *development*, structure outlives meaning. Elements are preserved even when their meaning is lost (conservatism), or when they have become detached from their original limited place and purpose, acquiring new and broader meanings in the process (universalization). And elements are introduced which have no apparent relationship to others (arbitrariness).[74]

---

73. For more information on the mixed chalice, see Strout, "*Of Thine Own Have We Given Thee*," 86–87.
74. Taft, "Structural Analysis of Liturgical Units," 315.

The structure of liturgical rites provides the map. The liturgical historian can more effectively trace a rite's structure because structure persists through history even when the meanings change.

Anglicans understand this principle well due to the BCP. An Anglican can walk into any service around the globe and, even when not understanding the language being spoken, still recognize the service as Anglican due to its common structure. Ask any Anglican what some element of the service means, and you will receive many answers due to the comprehensiveness of the tradition. Ask any Anglican about the structure of the service, and you will receive a relatively consistent response.

However, attempting to study an entire liturgical rite structurally can be daunting, if not impossible. Therefore, Taft suggests comparing individual units that compose the full rite.[75] For example, the Eucharist includes an entrance rite, the Liturgy of the Word, the offertory, the Eucharistic Prayer, the communion rite, and the dismissal. Each of these units could be subdivided further. Comparing these units historically provides for a more accurate analysis because these units can evolve, move to different places in the rite, drop out of the rite, and return to it.

This chapter uses Taft's comparative analysis of liturgical units. Taft elucidates the importance of tracing a liturgical unit's history.

> One seeks to go back to that point at which the unit under study emerges in its pristine integrity, before decomposition set in. Decomposition is usually provoked by later additions. Overloaded rites like overloaded circuits eventually blow a fuse. Something has to be unplugged, and in liturgical load reducing the integrity of units is rarely respected, especially if their original form is no longer understood, or if they are

---

75. Taft, "Structural Analysis of Liturgical Units," 318.

no longer executed as they were originally intended to be. Observing how this happens to liturgical structures tells us something not only about the past, but also about the very dynamics of liturgical growth and change.[76]

Initially, one might think that this chapter focused on entire liturgical rites: baptism, confirmation, and the Eucharist. Due to the disintegration of the unitive rite of initiation into separate rites, this perspective is understandable. This chapter showed how the unitive rite of initiation became "overloaded" due to bishops' inability to maintain personal connections as the Church grew, parents' concerns for *quam primum* baptism for their infants, political and ecclesial leaders' desires to use liturgy for uniformity, and many other reasons. If we see baptism, anointings/hand-layings, and communion as units within an originally unitive rite, we have seen how "decomposition" has occurred. By using this method, we could more effectively map the evolution of the unitive rite, its disintegration, and reintegration.

Structure alone is not enough. After all, our liturgical rites have meanings even if those meanings have changed over time. We must interpret the data we have uncovered. After mapping the structure of the liturgical units and analyzing their historical development, we use that data to inform our interpretations today. How did this development change the meaning of the rites? Did new meanings get added and others lost?

Mapping the structure of liturgical rites reveals their historical evolution and provides important data for present-day interpretations, but it does not explain the purpose of this evolution. Why do the liturgical units evolve? Why do liturgies change over time? The answer involves many reasons.

---

76. Taft, "Structural Analysis of Liturgical Units," 324.

One reason can be seen in the interaction between liturgical rites and the cultures in which they occur. This interaction is known as inculturation. Another eminent liturgical scholar, Anscar Chupungco, defines inculturation as "the process whereby pertinent elements of a local culture are integrated into the texts, rites, symbols, and institutions employed by a local church for its worship."[77]

Chupungco begins with the process. Inculturation does not happen in a punctiliar fashion such as at the origin of a rite or its first introduction into a new culture. It is a process that is dynamic and ever-present. Just as liturgical history clearly shows that no "pure and pristine" liturgies have ever existed, it also shows that cultures have always influenced liturgical development. It would be equally unwise to believe that inculturation occurs only for "others." Just like no liturgical rites have endured through history unchanged, so no liturgical rites remain impervious to the cultures around them.

Inculturation also influences all aspects of liturgical rites. While liturgical texts may provide the most forthright data, other liturgical elements also experience inculturation. Inculturation affects the rites or the way worship occurs. It also influences symbols such as objects, art, music, and architecture, and it impacts the institutions or way in which liturgy is governed.

Thus, an important reason why liturgical units develop is inculturation. However, Chupungco argues that inculturation is more than just a historical process to be observed. It is also a conscious endeavor in which the Church must engage. He bases this theological claim on the incarnation of Christ.

> The incarnation is an historical event, but its mystery lives on whenever the Church assumes the social and cultural

---

77. Chupungco, "Liturgy and Inculturation," 339.

conditions of the people among whom she dwells. Adaptation is thus not an option, but a theological imperative arising from the incarnational exigency. The Church must incarnate herself in every race, as Christ incarnated himself in the Jewish race.[78]

Therefore, inculturation is a historical fact to be considered and a "theological imperative." The Church has always engaged in inculturation and must continue to do so.

Should the Church incorporate all cultural elements into its liturgical rites? Clearly, some elements should be avoided. Therefore, the principle of inculturation involves discernment. Cultural elements are not value-free but value-laden. Some of these values accord with the Gospel message of the Church, and some do not. The Church must discern which cultural elements to include in its liturgical rites and from which to refrain. Of course, these values will also evolve; thus, liturgical inculturation remains ever-evolving.

Our analysis of the unitive rite of initiation provided a significant amount of data. Much more data exists. We focused on the evolution of ecclesiological symbolism in these rites. We saw how symbols surrounding baptism and the Eucharist in the early church were rich in ecclesiological import. While the remission of sins had always played a part in baptism, other symbols, such as anointing and vesture in a white garment and stole, included rich ecclesiological imagery.

In addition to these symbols, Paul, Irenaeus, Cyprian, and Augustine also stressed the unity of the Church through baptism and the Eucharist. This emphasis on unity was important as the Church adapted to the Greco-Roman culture, the ever-present reality of persecution, and the poignant impact of martyrdom. The church must remain united to resist these cultural forces.

---

78. Chupungco, *Cultural Adaptation of the Liturgy*, 59.

In its early years, initiation into the Church was one complete contiguous event that included a possible pre-baptismal anointing, the baptism itself, a possible post-baptismal anointing, and then the reception of communion. This unified initiatory rite would endure in the Church for centuries. The beginning of the disintegration of this unified initiatory rite had its roots in the early medieval period, grew in the high medieval period, and continued in the Reformation period.

Alongside this disintegration of the initiatory rite was the rise in *quam primum* infant baptism that developed as the theology of original sin spread in the Western Church. Baptism became primarily about the exorcism of original sin and lost much of its ecclesiological symbolism.

In addition, eucharistic realism increased the importance of the reception of communion, which led to further required preparation before receiving communion. It also led to increased clericalism as the priest became the sole person responsible for consecrating the elements. Eventually, this increased clericalism resulted in Pope Gregory VII centralizing authority in the papacy. The increase in eucharistic realism and the pope's primacy contributed to the Church's fracturing in the sixteenth-century reformations. While eucharistic realism and clericalism were the subjects of much debate in the sixteenth-century reformations, the baptismal and eucharistic rites within the Church of England continued to be separated and emphasized an exorcistic and penitential theology.

During the contemporary period, the ecumenical and liturgical movements profoundly affected the liturgy of The Episcopal Church. Through a series of prayer book studies and trial liturgies, the revisers of the prayer book attempted to gauge how a return to a unified initiatory rite would be accepted within The Episcopal Church. In the end, it was accepted with provisions. Baptism is full initiation into the Church. However, confirmation continues as an episcopally sanctioned public affirmation of faith. Thus, the reunification of the initiatory rites had only just begun. The next chapter looks more closely at these contemporary rites in The Episcopal Church.

CHAPTER THREE

BAPTISM, THE EUCHARIST, AND THE LITURGY OF THE CHURCH
A Baptismal-Eucharistic Liturgical Theology

In the last chapter, we traced the history of baptism and the Eucharist through the Church's practice and showed their ecclesiological implications. The closer the Church linked baptism and the Eucharist, the stronger it linked their ecclesiological implications. The desire to return to this ancient paradigm began in The Episcopal Church's efforts to reunite the initiatory rites of baptism, confirmation, and the Eucharist. While this reunification did not take place completely, the return of baptism to an ecclesiological center in The Episcopal Church was evident in the 1979 revision of the BCP. In this chapter, we look more closely at the 1979 BCP to reveal the inherent baptismal-eucharistic liturgical theology it expresses.

Liturgical scholars advocate for a two-part methodology for studying liturgical theology.[1] The first part is the historical study of the liturgical rites, and the second part is a theological reflection on the experiences of those rites. To study the liturgy historically, one must first understand the Ordo or structure. Schmemann makes a

---

1. See Schmemann, *Introduction to Liturgical Theology*, 81-81; Kavanaugh, *On Liturgical Theology*, 131; Taft, "Liturgy as Theology," 115-116; Fagerburg, *Theologia Prima*, 40-41.

fundamental claim that "the elucidation of the content of the Ordo and its place in the liturgical tradition of the Church constitutes the primary task of liturgical theology."[2] The liturgy is not a collection of piecemeal items that can be mixed and matched as one pleases. The liturgy is, by its very nature, a structure. This structure has important theological meaning. Therefore, our first task will be to look at the structure of the 1979 BCP compared to previous versions.

Then, using Taft's methodology, discussed at the end of chapter two, we will compare specific units within the liturgy in their historical context.[3] We will look at units within the 1979 BCP in greater detail and compare them against previous versions of the BCP. We will see that the revisers of the 1979 BCP integrated baptism firmly within the context of the Eucharist while simultaneously reincorporating baptismal themes into the Eucharist. They saw these rites as a unified whole that cannot be shuffled around without grave theological implications. Therefore, our second task will be to illuminate the baptismal-eucharistic liturgical theology of the 1979 BCP.

Finally, we will conclude this chapter with theological reflection based on the liturgical data gleaned that illustrates the baptismal-eucharistic liturgical theology of the 1979 BCP. We will use Gordon Lathrop's model of juxtaposition to guide an example of *theologia secunda*.[4] Like Schmemann and Taft, Lathrop emphasizes the importance of structure. By juxtaposing seemingly disparate objects, he argues that new meaning can emerge.[5] We will explore these new meanings and their ecclesiological implications.

---

2. Schmemann, *Introduction to Liturgical Theology*, 33.

3. Taft, *Beyond East and West*, 154.

4. See the Diving Deeper section below for a further discussion on *theologia prima* and *theologia secunda*.

5. Lathrop, *Holy Things*, 27-33.

The Ordo: Structure and Meaning

Schmemann provides a basic definition of the Ordo as "the collection of rules and prescriptions ('rubrics' in the language of Western liturgics) which regulate the Church's worship."[6] He recognizes two inherent problems that can arise when studying the Ordo. The first problem is a tendency toward rubrical fundamentalism in which the rules and regulations of the Ordo become immutable and absolute law. The other problem is indifference when the Ordo becomes meaningless in and of itself. It acts merely as a container of various liturgical parts that can be used in any order as desired. Schmemann clarifies the task of liturgical theology as "find[ing] the Ordo behind the 'rubrics,' regulations and rules—to find the unchanging principle, the living norm or 'logos' of worship as a whole, within what is accidental and temporary."[7] Our aim in looking at the structure of the 1979 BCP is to find that "living norm or 'logos' of worship as a whole." We will uncover that "logos" through a careful look at the structure of the 1979 BCP and show that the revisers intended for baptism and the Eucharist to form the ecclesiological center of the Ordo.

The first and most obvious redaction to the Ordo in the 1979 BCP was the placement of the rite of Baptism within the BCP itself. Previous versions of the BCP placed the rite of baptism in the same section of the prayer book as other pastoral rites, such as confirmation, matrimony, and burial. The 1979 BCP places it under its own heading before the Holy Eucharist.[8] As noted in chapter two, the Committee on the Contents and Order of the Draft Proposed Book specifically suggested this change in placement, which is highly significant as it

---

6. Schmemann, *Introduction to Liturgical Theology*, 33.

7. Schmemann, *Introduction to Liturgical Theology*, 39. See also, Denysenko, "Renewing Alexander Schmemann's Liturgical Legacy," 179-181.

8. Marshall, *Prayer Book Parallels*, 1:54-57.

recognizes that baptism is not one of several pastoral offices but a rite that forms one of the cornerstones of The Episcopal Church's liturgy.

The 1979 BCP distinguishes the purpose of baptism with the following rubric at the beginning of the rite: "Holy Baptism is full initiation by water and the Holy Spirit into Christ's Body, the Church." By adding this rubric, the editors of the 1979 BCP signaled baptism's central role in the Church. Confirmation was no longer required to be a full member. Baptism is sufficient.

The next rubric continues, "Holy Baptism is appropriately administered within the Eucharist as the chief service on a Sunday or other feast."[9] Previous versions of the BCP suggested that it is "most convenient" to perform baptism on a Sunday in the public service of the Church. However, they made no specific connection with the eucharistic service. Thus, Morning Prayer often became the context for baptism. The 1979 BCP, on the other hand, explicitly draws the connection between baptism and the Eucharist.

Is the placement of baptism before the Eucharist in ordering the rites enough to suggest that baptism must precede receiving communion? No rubric in the prayer book requires that baptism precede the reception of communion.[10] If the desired approach to the rubrics was one using a fundamentalist spirit, then the lack of such a rubric might be disturbing. However, the purpose of the Ordo is not to prescribe or restrict action in a legalistic fashion. The purpose of the Ordo is to reveal the underlying "logos" of worship. Therefore, the placement of the rite of baptism before the rite of the Eucharist and yet simultaneously within the rite of the Eucharist signifies the desire of the revisers to reunify these initiatory rites.

---

9. Marshall, *Prayer Book Parallels*, 1:54-57.

10. The canons of The Episcopal Church do require it, however. The Canons of the Episcopal Church (Title 1.17.7).

Another set of rubrics found in the "Additional Directions" of the baptismal rite also suggests ecclesiological implications for baptism. In this section, the rubrics state, "Holy Baptism is especially appropriate at the Easter Vigil, on the Day of Pentecost, on All Saints' Day or the Sunday after All Saints' Day, and on the Feast of the Baptism of our Lord (the First Sunday after the Epiphany). It is recommended that, as far as possible, Baptisms be reserved for these occasions or when a bishop is present."[11] Marion Hatchett believes that these five occasions have theological importance:

> The Easter Vigil, which signifies baptism as death and resurrection—the Pauline emphasis; the Day of Pentecost, which signifies baptism as the receiving of the Holy Spirit—the Lukan emphasis; the first Sunday after the Epiphany: The Baptism of our Lord, which signifies baptism as new birth, regeneration—the Johannine emphasis; All Saints' Day or the Sunday after All Saints' Day, which signifies baptism as the reception into the communion of saints; and the time of the visitation of the bishop, which signifies baptism as the reception into the holy catholic church.[12]

Hatchett gives All Saints' Day and the bishop's visitation specific ecclesiological meaning. In addition, because Pentecost is often understood as commemorating the birth of the Church, baptism on that day signifies the connection between baptism and the Church. Furthermore, as noted in chapter two, the connection between the baptism of Jesus and the later rite of baptism also had clear ecclesiological implications for the early church. Thus, four of the

---

11. Marshall, *Prayer Book Parallels*, 1:265.
12. Hatchett, *Commentary on the American Prayer Book*, 267-268.

five holy days in which the celebration of baptism is "especially appropriate" contain ecclesiological connections.

The Ordo of the 1979 BCP does not prescribe that baptism precede the reception of communion through a rubrical mandate. To do so would be to overstep the purpose of the Ordo. Church canons are meant to prescribe and restrict explicit behavior. The Ordo, on the other hand, is meant to illuminate the underlying "logos" of worship. However, the interwoven connection that the Ordo makes between baptism and the Eucharist, along with the connections with the appropriate holy days, illuminate the strong ecclesiological implications for baptism and the Eucharist within the 1979 BCP.

Comparing Liturgical Units: Content and Meaning

A comparison of specific units within the Ordo with previous versions of the BCP shows a marked trend toward centralizing baptism and the Eucharist as the foundation for the liturgical theology of the 1979 BCP. Furthermore, ecclesiology plays an important role in this baptismal-eucharistic liturgical theology.

The beginning of the baptismal rite in the 1979 BCP reveals an important difference from previous versions. The rite in the 1979 BCP begins with the standard opening proclamation from the rite for Holy Eucharist. After the opening proclamation,

The Celebrant then continues
　　　　　　　There is one Body and one Spirit;
People　　　There is one hope in God's call to us;
Celebrant　 One Lord, One Faith, one Baptism;
People　　　One God and Father of all.[13]

---

13. Marshall, *Prayer Book Parallels*, 1:237.

The baptismal rite is already setting up the ecclesiology of "One Body." The stress placed on unity in this portion of the baptismal rite also has important ecumenical implications. As an explicit statement of unity, this proclamation informs The Episcopal Church's ecumenical partners that it believes in shared baptism. We will discuss these ecumenical implications further in chapter five.

The next section of the baptismal rite regarding the presentation of the candidates has changed in the 1979 BCP through omissions from previous versions. The previous revisions of the BCP included long exhortations about the purpose of baptism. The first exhortation found in the 1662, 1789, 1892, and 1928 versions of the BCP includes a specific ecclesiological reference. It states: "that *he* may be baptized with Water and the Holy Ghost, and received into Christ's holy Church, and be made a living member of the same."[14] However, the overarching theme in these exhortations is the remission of sins and the reception of eternal life. The exhortation strongly emphasizes the individual candidate's salvation. The elimination of these exhortations in the 1979 BCP indicates more emphasis on the corporate nature of baptism and less on its individual soteriological benefits.

After the traditional renunciations and adhesions, another significant change occurs in the 1979 BCP with the addition of the Baptismal Covenant. In previous versions of the BCP, only the candidates (or their sponsors) were asked questions regarding their faith. However, the 1979 BCP instructs everyone in the congregation to say the Baptismal Covenant, not just the candidates or their sponsors.[15] This congregational response also emphasizes the corporate nature of this rite. Of course, one cannot assume that every person in the congregation is baptized. However, the implied

---

14. Marshall, *Prayer Book Parallels*, 1:240-241.
15. Marshall, *Prayer Book Parallels*, 1:249.

assumption in this congregational response is that the body responding is a baptized body renewing their own Baptismal Covenant in solidarity with the candidates who are about to be baptized. Just as the opening proclamation states, that body is "One Body," and it is a baptized and baptizing body. Thus, the 1979 BCP's inclusion of the Baptismal Covenant emphasizes baptism as a corporate and public event involving the whole Church rather than an individual and private ceremony for just the family.

The Baptismal Covenant initially follows the same format as the Apostles' Creed but in an interrogatory pattern. It continues after the Creed with the question, "Will you continue in the apostles' teaching and fellowship, in the breaking of bread, and in the prayers?"[16] This question follows the Ordo in Peter's sermon at Pentecost (Acts 2:42). This Ordo begins with the apostles proclaiming the Word of God and baptizing those who believe. Then the newly baptized "continue in the apostles' teaching and fellowship, in the breaking of bread, and in the prayers." This reference to the breaking of bread and the prayers is a eucharistic reference. The Baptismal Covenant continues with a missiological emphasis on proclaiming the Good News of God in Christ through word and example, being willing to seek and serve Christ in all persons, and striving for justice and peace among all people while respecting the dignity of every human being. This missiological emphasis within the Baptismal Covenant has become the lynchpin of many of the social justice movements of The Episcopal Church. By referencing the Baptismal Covenant, these social justice movements call on the entire Church to respond to these missiological imperatives. Thus, they illustrate the ecclesiological implications of baptism in the 1979 BCP.

---

16. Marshall, *Prayer Book Parallels*, 1:251.

The Thanksgiving over Water invokes additional ecclesiological images. This prayer draws historical parallels with the children of Israel passing through the Red Sea and the baptism of Jesus by John. It continues with the Romans 6 baptismal theology of death to sin and resurrection to new life. However, it does not capitalize on that theology as previous versions have. Instead, it concludes with, "Therefore in joyful obedience to your Son, we bring into his fellowship those who come to him in faith, baptizing them in the Name of the Father, and of the Son, and of the Holy Spirit."[17] Thus, this rite describes baptism not only as a remission of sin and a gift of eternal life but also as a bringing into the fellowship of Christ's body. The words "bring into" imply a movement from outside Christ's fellowship into Christ's fellowship. Thus, baptism, not the Eucharist, is the initiation into Christ's fellowship.

The next important event is the consignation with optional chrismation. The previous versions of the BCP include the consignation but with a different emphasis. These versions recognize the candidate's reception "into the Congregation of Christ's flock." Still, the consignation itself is meant to strengthen the candidate to combat Satan and the world and to stand up for the faith of Christ.[18] The 1979 BCP, on the other hand, says very simply but significantly, "*N.*, you are sealed by the Holy Spirit in Baptism and marked as Christ's own for ever. *Amen.*"[19] As discussed in chapter two, this sealing of the Spirit, along with chrismation, had historical importance as the precursor for what later became the rite of confirmation. Again, the revisers are signifying with the inclusion of this ritual action in the baptismal rite rather than in the confirmation rite that only one rite is necessary to fully initiate someone into Christ's Body.

---

17. Marshall, *Prayer Book Parallels*, 1:255.
18. Marshall, *Prayer Book Parallels*, 1:256-257.
19. Marshall, *Prayer Book Parallels*, 1:256-257.

The rite continues as the Celebrant and people welcome the newly baptized by saying, "We receive you into the household of God. Confess the faith of Christ crucified, proclaim his resurrection, and share with us in his eternal priesthood."[20] The revisers have again proclaimed the ecclesiological connections in baptism. This reception into the household of God presupposes that, in some way, the candidates were not formerly a part of the household of God— or at least not recognized as such by the gathered congregation. However, now, through baptism, the congregation recognizes them as full members of the household of God. Furthermore, this rite once again proclaims the "eternal priesthood" of believers like in the early Church. These newly ordained priests in the Church will join with all the other priests in the congregation as the service continues with the celebration of the Holy Eucharist.

Before examining the rite of Holy Eucharist, we will consider the Exhortation. Previous versions of the BCP embedded the Exhortation into the eucharistic rite itself. The Exhortation was much longer and included three different versions for different occasions. The 1979 BCP retains the Exhortation but places it as a prefatory rite before the actual rite of the Eucharist. The rubric for it is a permissive rubric stating that it "may be used, in whole or in part, either during the Liturgy or at other times."[21] Like its predecessors, this Exhortation also calls the participants to prepare themselves for communion based on Paul's injunction (1 Cor. 11:29). In contrast, some proponents of communion without baptism suggest that persons need no preparation before receiving communion; the 1979 BCP suggests otherwise.[22]

---

20. Marshall, *Prayer Book Parallels*, 1:256-257.
21. 1979BCP, 316-317.
22. cf. Edmonson, 220-221.

As we consider the eucharistic rite, we will not step through it with the same detailed precision that we did the baptismal rite. We have already shown the interconnection between these rites as the baptismal rite normatively occurs in the context of the Eucharist. The baptismal rite and the eucharistic rite were joined together in the 1979 BCP, unlike their predecessors. In this section, however, we will highlight changes and additions to the eucharistic rite of the 1979 BCP that further connect it with baptism and draw upon its ecclesiological implications.

First, the proper prefaces provide an example. Proper prefaces are a particularity of the Western rite. The celebrant uses a proper preface to introduce the specific intention for the eucharistic service. The 1549 BCP included only five proper prefaces for Christmas, Easter, Ascension, Pentecost, and Trinity Sunday. The 1928 BCP added three new prefaces: Epiphany, the Purification, Annunciation, and Transfiguration [one preface for all three commemorations], and All Saints. Finally, the 1979 BCP increased the proper prefaces to twenty-two.[23] We will examine the baptismal theology that some of these proper prefaces convey within the rite of the Eucharist itself.

The 1979 BCP makes an important change to the proper preface for Pentecost. The second half of the preface states "uniting peoples of many tongues in the confession of one faith, and giving to your Church the power to serve you as a royal priesthood, and to preach the Gospel to all nations."[24] The previous versions did not include any statement about the Church serving as a "royal priesthood." This reference to the "royal priesthood" connects the Eucharist with the baptismal rite's final welcome of the baptized into the "eternal priesthood." Furthermore, the 1979 BCP lists Pentecost as one of the

---

23. Hatchett, *Commentary on the American Prayer Book*, 397-398.
24. Marshall, *Prayer Book Parallels*, 1:357.

days on which baptism is "especially appropriate." Thus, the revisers connected baptism, the Eucharist, and the Church with this proper preface.

Other proper prefaces include similar baptismal and ecclesiological connections. For example, the third proper preface of the Lord's Day, "Of God the Holy Spirit," states, "Who by water and the Holy Spirit has made us a new people in Jesus Christ our Lord, to show forth your glory in all the world."[25] The reference to water and the Holy Spirit signifies the connection between the bath and the sealing of the Holy Spirit found in the baptismal rite. These connected activities make the Church "a new people in Jesus Christ our Lord."

Of course, the proper preface for baptism also has ecclesiological implications: "Because in Jesus Christ our Lord you have received us as your sons and daughters, made us citizens of your kingdom, and given us the Holy Spirit to guide us into all truth."[26] The revisers are once again unifying confirmation with baptism in this preface by declaring that God gives the Holy Spirit in baptism, not confirmation. No further initiatory rites are necessary. Baptism is full initiation into the Church.

The Eucharistic Prayers themselves have rich ecclesiological implications. Eucharistic Prayer C contains the only explicit baptismal reference in the Eucharistic Prayers: "And so, Father, we who have been redeemed by him, and made a new people by water and the Spirit, now bring before you these gifts. Sanctify them by your Holy Spirit to be the Body and the Blood of Jesus Christ our Lord."[27] The invocation of the Holy Spirit, or epiclesis, found in the other Eucharistic Prayers, while not having the specific baptismal reference as in Prayer C,

---

25. Marshall, *Prayer Book Parallels*, 1:355.
26. Marshall, *Prayer Book Parallels*, 1:361.
27. Marshall, *Prayer Book Parallels*, 1:401.

nonetheless also emphasizes the congregation reconstituting as one body again. Eucharistic Prayer A says, "Sanctify us also that we may faithfully receive this holy Sacrament, and serve you in unity, constancy, and peace . . ."[28] Eucharistic Prayer B says, "Unite us to your Son in his sacrifice, that we may be acceptable through him, being sanctified by the Holy Spirit . . . through Jesus Christ our Lord, the firstborn of all creation, the head of the Church, and the author of our salvation."[29] The epiclesis of Eucharistic Prayer C includes this unity as mentioned above, and later, the prayer reinforces the unity of one body again with "Let the grace of this Holy Communion make us one body, one spirit in Christ, that we may worthily serve the world in his name."[30] Eucharistic Prayer D says, "Grant that all who share this bread and cup may become one body and one spirit, a living sacrifice in Christ, to the praise of your Name."[31] Even the Order for Eucharist, Form 1, says, "Gather us by this Holy Communion into one body in your Son Jesus Christ."[32] All of these Eucharistic Prayers emphasize becoming one body in Christ. This one body is the Church as Paul teaches in Romans 12. Thus, these Eucharistic Prayers connect the Eucharist with the Church.

Taken out of the context of the Ordo of the 1979 BCP, these Eucharistic Prayers might give one the impression that they are initiatory in nature. They all emphasize that the congregation will become one body through the Eucharist. However, these prayers are not speaking of initiation, but rather of reconstitution. The Eucharist does not make the Church a new people. Baptism makes the Church

---

28. Marshall, *Prayer Book Parallels*, 1:402.
29. Marshall, *Prayer Book Parallels*, 1:402.
30. Marshall, *Prayer Book Parallels*, 1:403.
31. Marshall, *Prayer Book Parallels*, 1:403.
32. Marshall, *Prayer Book Parallels*, 1:403.

a new people by water and the Spirit, as Prayer C indicates. However, the Eucharist does reconstitute the Church as one body. Baptism initially makes the Church one body, but then sin separates members of the Church from Christ and from their neighbors. The Eucharist reconstitutes the Body of Christ through the power of the Holy Spirit. Here again, the Ordo displays the unity of baptism, the Eucharist, and the Church.

After the eucharistic prayer and right before the distribution of communion is another important addition in the 1979 BCP: the *Sancta sanctis*, or "the holy for the holy." The actual words in the rite are "The Gifts of God for the People of God." These words come from fourth-century Eastern liturgies.[33] Again, the rite emphasizes the Eucharist's corporate nature. It is not simply a gift for individual salvation. Instead, it is for "the People of God," and these people of God understand their identity through baptism, where they are "received into the household of God."

After the distribution of communion, the congregation joins in saying the Postcommunion Prayer. The Rite 2 service of the 1979 BCP adds a Postcommunion Prayer, but it also retains the prayer that has been used since 1549, updating it with contemporary language. Both prayers emphasize the ecclesiological implications of the Eucharist. The prayer shared since 1549 says:

> Almighty and everliving God, we thank you for feeding us with the spiritual food of the most precious Body and Blood of your Son our Saviour Jesus Christ; and for assuring us in these holy mysteries that we are living members of the Body of your Son and heirs of your eternal kingdom.[34]

---

33. Hatchett, *Commentary on the American Prayer Book*, 383.
34. Hatchett, *Commentary on the American Prayer Book*, 373-375.

Through the Eucharist, the Church becomes again "living members of the Body of your Son." Here is the imagery of "One Body" yet again. The new Postcommunion Prayer in the 1979 BCP Rite 2 uses this imagery as well: "Eternal God, heavenly Father, you have graciously accepted us as living members of your Son our Savior Jesus Christ . . ."[35] These prayers allude not only to the Sacrament as the Body of Christ but also to the Church as the Body of Christ. Thus, the congregation acknowledges that the Eucharist has reconstituted it as the Body of Christ, the Church, through the Sacrament.

Again, without considering the rest of the Ordo, one might consider these prayers as initiatory in nature, but they are not. One cannot separate the rites of baptism and the Eucharist. They are one unified rite. Like the Eucharistic Prayers, the Postcommunion Prayers in the Eucharist speak of the reconstitution of the Body of Christ through the power of the Holy Spirit in the Eucharist. However, they draw upon the indissoluble bond between baptism and the Eucharist in the Holy Spirit. Just as the Holy Spirit joins each person with the one body of Christ in baptism, the Holy Spirit reconstitutes that one body in the Eucharist.

In addition to the rites of baptism and the Eucharist, the rites found in the Pastoral Offices highlight the baptismal-eucharistic liturgical theology of the 1979 BCP. While the 1979 BCP places Confirmation, Reception, and Reaffirmation of Baptismal Vows within the context of the baptismal rite, it also provides separate rites in the Pastoral Offices section.[36] Of course, the candidates must be baptized to participate in any of these rites, and the rite itself is normatively included in the context of the Eucharist. In the

---

35. Hatchett, *Commentary on the American Prayer Book*, 373-375.
36. 1979BCP, 309-310 and 412-419, respectively.

rite for Marriage, the 1979 BCP includes a new rubric which states, "In The Episcopal Church it is required that one, at least, of the parties must be a baptized Christian...."[37] Again, the normative service for the Marriage rite is the Eucharist. As for the burial rite, the 1662, 1786, 1789, and 1892 BCPs included an exclusive rubric: "Here is to be noted, that the Office ensuing is not to be used for any unbaptized Adults...."[38] However, the 1928 BCP loosened this rubric by removing reference to baptism and stating, "It is to be noted that this Office is appropriate to be used only for the faithful departed in Christ...."[39] The 1979 BCP has no restrictive rubric regarding the burial service. However, it reinserts mention of baptism with "Baptized Christians are properly buried from the church. The service should be held at a time when the congregation can be present."[40] The normative service is again the Eucharist. The point here is not that the services of marriage and burial are restricted to only the baptized but rather they would normatively involve the baptized and be corporate in nature.

Thus, the 1979 BCP recognizes the corporate nature of baptism and the Eucharist. Rather than seeing baptism restrictively, the 1979 BCP sees it descriptively. God first incorporated the person into the one Body of the Church at baptism and continually reconstitutes that person into the one Body through the Eucharist. Thus, baptism and the Eucharist interpenetrate the entire liturgical theology of the 1979 BCP with strong ecclesiological implications.

---

37. Marshall, *Prayer Book Parallels*, 1:439.
38. Marshall, *Prayer Book Parallels*, 1:530.
39. Marshall, *Prayer Book Parallels*, 1:531.
40. Marshall, *Prayer Book Parallels*, 1:531.

Juxtaposition: Breaking Open Meaning

Thus far, our procedure for explicating the liturgical theology of the 1979 BCP has been quite straightforward. First, we looked at the Ordo as a whole and noticed the placement of the baptismal rite before the eucharistic rite, with each rite interpenetrating the other. Next, we looked at liturgical units within the baptismal and eucharistic rites and the other Pastoral Offices that interconnect baptism, the Eucharist, and the Church. In this section, rather than highlighting the interconnections among the rites, we will break them open through juxtaposition.

In his book *Holy Things: A Liturgical Theology*, Gordon Lathrop stresses the importance of juxtaposition in breaking open new meaning.

> In a broken myth the terms of the myth and its power to evoke our own experience of the world remain, but the coherent language of the myth is seen as insufficient and its power to hold and create as equivocal. The myth is both true and at the same time wrong, capable of truth only by reference to a new thing, beyond its own terms. Such a break is present in the deep intention of the words and ritual practices of the liturgy: the old is maintained; yet, by means of juxtaposition and metaphor, the old is made to speak the new.[41]

Like Schmemann, Taft, and other liturgical theologians, Lathrop also stresses the importance of structure within the liturgy. Lathrop highlights the comparison of liturgical units as set one against the other. For example, the Eucharist juxtaposes Word and Table.[42] The

---

41. Lathrop, *Holy Things*, 27.
42. Lathrop, *Holy Things*, 43-53.

eucharistic service begins with the Liturgy of the Word in which the congregation reads Scripture and prays. Then, it moves to the Liturgy of the Table or Holy Communion.

Similarly, baptism juxtaposes teaching and bath.[43] As discussed in chapter two, the early church stressed a catechumenal process before baptism. As church history continued and infant baptism became the norm, the Church shifted the catechumenate to after baptism. The liturgical movement of the twentieth century has attempted to reorient this order to its original state. The juxtapositions within these rites break open new meaning for the Church.

However, juxtaposition is not meant just for breaking open new meaning but also for creating tension. For example, Lathrop recognizes the inherent tension between baptism and the Eucharist.

> The word *baptism* is used for the whole complex of teaching and bath. Or, rather, since the bath washes one clean for participation in this community, the word *baptism* is most properly used for the complex of teaching, bath, and meal. We teach, then we wash, and then we lead to the common meal.[44]

Lathrop stresses that the Church must keep the tension created by these juxtapositions in play. When the Church separates the units from each other, the units lose that tension.

The disintegration of the initiatory rite during the late medieval and reformation periods exemplifies this loss of tension. As the Church separated the rite, it lost much of the ecclesiological meaning of the unified rite. Instead, the Church saw baptism as primarily a rite of exorcism for original sin, and the Eucharist was only available to those who were worthy to receive it. The Church then used confirmation

---

43. Lathrop, *Holy Things*, 59-68.
44. Lathrop, *Holy Things*, 61.

to establish whether a person was indeed "worthy" or not. In the meantime, the Church lost the rich ecclesiological symbolism of the newly baptized being sealed in the Spirit, anointed with oil, made a priest of the Church, and immediately led into celebrating the Eucharist.

Juxtaposing baptism and the Eucharist reveals additional ecclesiological images through water. While water invokes the image of bathing—that which was dirty becoming clean—it also provides additional imagery. Beyond Lathrop's bath and meal images, we will consider three more images in the Thanksgiving over Water found in the 1979 BCP that break open additional ecclesiological meanings: chaos/creation, liberation/thanksgiving, and anointing/mission.

The Thanksgiving over Water begins, "We thank you, Almighty God, for the gift of water. Over it the Holy Spirit moved in the beginning of creation."[45] Here, one sees chaos and creation. These images reach back into the farthest corners of humanity's ancestral minds, recalling images of the great abyss. Many ancient mythologies begin with the roiling waters of chaos. The Judeo-Christian tradition speaks of "a wind from God swept over the face of the waters (Gen 1:2)." The Hebrew word for "wind" is *ruach*, which also means "spirit." The spirit of God moves over the chaotic waters of creation.

In the Eucharist, we also see a connection with creation. A traditional prayer by the celebrant when the bread and wine are offered coincides with this image of creation from chaos: "All things come of thee, O Lord, and of thine own have we given thee (1 Chron. 29:14 KJV)." In the Eucharist, the Church offers back to God that which God created from chaos in thanksgiving to God. This offering is a corporate act of the entire Church. While each person individually may contribute to the restoration of creation, the Church has a role

---

45. 1979BCP, 306.

to play as well. These images from baptism and the Eucharist remind the Church of that important ecological role.

In addition to restoring creation, the Church seeks to liberate the oppressed, as the next image indicates: "Through [water] you led the children of Israel out of their bondage in Egypt into the land of promise."[46] Here, we see liberation and thanksgiving. The children of Israel flee their Egyptian oppressors through the waters of the Red Sea. On the other side, they rejoice with one of the most ancient hymns in Scripture, the Song of Moses in Exodus 15: "I will sing to the Lord, for he has triumphed gloriously; horse and rider he has thrown into the sea." Water liberated the children of Israel. The Church also celebrates its liberation from sin and death in the Eucharist. At The Breaking of the Bread, the assembly says,

> Christ our Passover is sacrificed for us;
> *Therefore let us keep the feast.*[47]

Here is the image of Christ as the Paschal Lamb, which hearkens back to the children of Israel's escape from the oppressors. Through the Paschal Lamb, the children of Israel avoid the death of the firstborn that plagues their oppressors and finally leads to their liberation. In the Eucharist, Christ as the Paschal Lamb is present with us. Like the children of Israel rejoicing after coming through the Red Sea, the Church rejoices in the feast of the Risen Lamb. These images of liberation and thanksgiving remind the Church of its vocation to proclaim the end of the oppression of sin and death throughout the world.

The Thanksgiving over Water continues, "In it your Son Jesus received the baptism of John and was anointed by the Holy Spirit as

---

46. 1979BCP, 306.
47. 1979BCP, 364.

the Messiah, the Christ, to lead us, through his death and resurrection, from the bondage of sin into everlasting life."[48] Here, we see anointing and mission. The prayer draws the parallel between the baptism of Christ in the Jordan by John and our baptism. As John lifts Jesus out of the water, the Holy Spirit comes down and anoints him for ministry. The 1979 BCP draws upon this imagery through the sealing of the Spirit with optional chrismation in the baptismal rite. This anointing imagery hearkens back to the early Church's ecclesial imagery of the universal priesthood of all believers. Like Christ, the Holy Spirit anoints the baptismal candidate for public ministry.

The Eucharist also calls us to mission. At the end of the Eucharist, the deacon, as that order of ministry that especially connects the Church with mission in the world, dismisses the congregation to continue its public ministry out in the world:

Deacon   Let us go forth into the world,
           rejoicing in the power of the Spirit.
People   Thanks be to God.[49]

The Holy Spirit does not anoint members of the Church to be "pure" or special in some way. The Holy Spirit anoints them for service in the world. From the world, they enter the Church through baptism and the Eucharist and then return to the world—this is the Ordo of the 1979 BCP.

The images of chaos/creation, liberation/thanksgiving, and anointing/mission find their tension in the juxtaposition of baptism and the Eucharist. However, the Church feels that tension most strongly when considering these rites in their unity. Without baptism,

---

48. 1979BCP, 306.
49. 1979BCP, 366.

the images in the Eucharist become static. Creation appears without the underlying energy of chaos. The Church gives thanksgiving without recognizing its liberation and then is sent out on a mission but with no initial anointing from the Holy Spirit. Without the juxtaposition of baptism, these images in the Eucharist lose their inherent tension.

Communion without Baptism: Misunderstood Meanings

When we consider the Ordo of the 1979 BCP, compare liturgical units within baptism and the Eucharist, and recognize their meanings through juxtaposition, we see a baptismal-eucharistic liturgical theology emerge. The editors of the current prayer book sought to reunify the initiatory rites of baptism, consignation/chrismation, and the Eucharist. They did so not only for historical purposes to restore the ancient model but also for theological purposes. Baptism initiates one into the Body of Christ, the Church. The Eucharist reconstitutes the Body of Christ and sends it out in mission to the world.

Proponents of communion without baptism seek to change this baptismal-eucharistic liturgical theology of the prayer book. In his book *Liturgical Theology Revisited: Open Table, Baptism, Church*, Stephen Edmonson argues for a reversal of the traditional Ordo. He suggests that the reception of communion *should* precede baptism.[50]

Initially, Edmonson's position may appear indifferent to the Ordo, believing that the liturgy includes units that may be mixed and matched without care for the underlying *logos*. The desire to

---

50. Edmonson, *Liturgical Theology Revisited*, 17.

remain pastorally sensitive in allowing unbaptized persons to receive communion may fall into this category. Indeed, the Ordo should be flexible enough to permit pastoral responses when necessary. No one suggests checking baptismal certificates at the communion rail.

However, Edmonson insists that pastoral flexibility with the Ordo is insufficient. The Ordo must change. Full participation in the Eucharist, including reception of communion, must precede baptism. He desires a permanent change to the Ordo, and he does so for explicitly theological reasons.[51]

Edmonson recognizes the close relationship between baptism and the Eucharist in his theological discussion. "[The practice of open table] is, moreover, bound intimately to a second Christological practice, that of baptism, through which the open table *comes to its fruition in our lives*."[52] Here, Edmonson bases his theology on the disintegrated initiatory rite rather than the unitive rite. For Edmonson, baptism and the Eucharist remain separate liturgical acts, now moved into a different order. The Eucharist creates the longing for God. Baptism fulfills that longing.[53]

Initially, we might believe that Edmonson follows theologians before him in rearranging the Ordo of initiation. After all, the Ordo began as a unitive rite with pre-baptismal and post-baptismal anointings and hand-layings. Eventually, it disintegrated into separate rites in the Western Church, but the original Ordo was still baptism-confirmation-communion. Eventually, that changed to baptism-first confession/first communion-confirmation for the later medieval church. Then, the churches of the Reformation rearranged it to baptism-confirmation-communion. Now, Edmonson advocates

---

51. Edmonson, *Liturgical Theology Revisited*, 16-18.
52. Edmonson, *Liturgical Theology Revisited*, 55, emphasis added.
53. Edmonson, *Liturgical Theology Revisited*, 56-61.

for communion-baptism-confirmation, but it is still a disintegrated rite.[54]

Interestingly, Edmonson recognizes a theological lacuna in his argument when discussing the Holy Spirit's role.

> My account of the Eucharist in the previous chapter was *notably deficient in its omission of the Spirit* from the discussion. This was not from neglect of the Spirit, however, but from the conviction that the Spirit's sacramental role is best understood through this conversation about baptism, especially given my claim above that we must understand baptism and Eucharist together. *Table and font are inextricably bound.*[55]

If table and font are inextricably bound, how does one come to the table first and then the font? If the chrismation at baptism is the sacramental sign of the giving of the Holy Spirit but the reception of communion is initiation, where is the Holy Spirit between communion and baptism?

Medieval theologians faced this dilemma in seeking to explain confirmation's role after baptism. They recognized that one cannot live a Christian life without the empowerment of the Holy Spirit. Thus, confirmation became about strengthening the Holy Spirit instead of giving it. Proponents of communion without baptism face this same theological question: Where is the Holy Spirit in the life of the Christian if communion without baptism is initiatory?

Edmonson also recognizes the importance of mission. However, in his original article, "Opening the Table: The Body of Christ and God's Prodigal Grace," he reverses the missional emphasis of baptism

---

54. Presumably, confirmation would come later. Edmonson does not discuss confirmation.

55. Edmonson, *Liturgical Theology Revisited*, 90, emphases added.

and the Eucharist when he states, "Baptism, instead [of Eucharist], joins one to the mission of the true Elder Son, as we are remade in his image."[56] As described above, the 1979 BCP sends the Church into mission in the world with the postcommunion prayers and dismissal from the Eucharist, and the baptismal liturgy includes words of welcome and reception into the Body of Christ. However, Edmonson argues that the Eucharist should be the rite of invitation, and baptism should be the rite of mission. This argument reverses the Ordo. In his proposed Ordo, each time the Church participates in the Eucharist, it repeats the invitation to join the Body of Christ. Then, it receives the call to mission only once at baptism. In contrast, the traditional Ordo issues the invitation once at baptism and the call to mission at each Eucharist.

Edmonson also discusses the ecclesiological implications of communion without baptism but appears to contradict himself. We will walk through a key quotation. First, he states, "Through this meal, we the community become a symbol of Christ blessed, broken, and shared. We become Christ's body, through which the alienated and broken can experience God's reconciling love."[57] This statement accords with what we have discussed as the Eucharist reconstituting the Body of Christ. However, Edmonson's next statement contradicts his original assertion about initiation. "(Note the distinction: In baptism, individuals are engrafted into Christ's body, the church, but it is in the Eucharist that the church as a community is constituted as Christ's body. Baptism, then, engrafts us into the body of Christ constituted by the Eucharist.)"[58] This statement appears to affirm the traditional Ordo. Baptism engrafts

---

56. Edmonson, "Opening the Table," 221.
57. Edmonson, *Liturgical Theology Revisited*, 123.
58. Edmonson, *Liturgical Theology Revisited*, 123.

one into the Body of Christ, which the Eucharist then constitutes, baptism then Eucharist.

A close reading of Edmonson's theology reveals that the Eucharist has two principal functions: first, to bring one into Jesus' fellowship through the table and then, after baptism, to constitute the body of Christ. Baptism provides the necessary pivot from fellowship with Jesus to full member of the Body of Christ. Again, though, his theology fails to explain the ecclesial status of one who has received communion but has not yet been baptized. Are they a member of the Body of Christ or not? The postcommunion prayers of the 1979 BCP state forthrightly that they are, as discussed above.

Beyond the theological concerns presented in this argument is a significant pastoral concern. Imagine for a moment that someone with little to no experience with Christianity was to walk into a church practicing communion without baptism. They encounter a warm greeting, enjoy lively music, hear a rousing sermon, and then receive an invitation to "a closer relationship with Jesus" by receiving communion. Following the others around them, they walk forward and receive communion. Moments later, they pray the postcommunion prayer with the rest of the congregation beginning, "Eternal God, heavenly Father, you have graciously accepted us as living members of your Son our Savior Jesus Christ . . ."[59]

"Living members? What does that mean? What have I just done?" they might wonder. For Edmonson, the answer would appear to be that they just had a moment of closer fellowship with Jesus. However, the prayer book is clear. They are now members of the Body of Christ. Were they aware of the importance of their decision to receive communion? Likely not if they only received a brief invitation to come forward for a "closer relationship with Jesus."

---

59. 1979BCP, 365.

The traditional Ordo communicates the commitment one makes to Christ first through baptism. Candidates for baptism are presented to the entire congregation. They recite the renunciations and adhesions. They join with the congregation in the Baptismal Covenant and participate in the baptism and consignation with optional chrismation. Then, they are led directly into the eucharistic assembly to receive communion as a new member of the Body of Christ.

Proponents of communion without baptism rightfully critique baptism as a purity rite. Reducing baptism to the exorcism of original sin created several theological challenges, which the Church continues to face. However, the solution is not to rearrange the Ordo, as had already been done. The solution is to return baptism, chrismation, and communion to a unitive initiation rite. The answer is the baptismal-eucharistic liturgical theology of the 1979 BCP.

Diving Deeper

After this thorough analysis of the liturgical texts of The Episcopal Church, we could easily believe that liturgy is primarily about texts. The texts are important for some Christian traditions, including The Episcopal Church. The 1979 BCP begins, "The Holy Eucharist, the principal act of Christian worship on the Lord's Day and other major Feasts, and Daily Morning and Evening Prayer, *as set forth in this book*, are the regular services appointed for public worship in this Church."[60] Unlike some other Christian traditions, The Episcopal Church

---

60. 1979BCP, 13, emphasis added. The General Convention has authorized additional liturgical rites for trial use such as the *Enriching Our Worship* series. By the time of publication, it is highly likely that the General Convention will have passed an amendment to the Constitution giving these trial rites a path to equal status as the prayer book.

prescribes only authorized texts for public worship. Furthermore, clergy promise in their ordination vows to "be loyal to the doctrine, discipline, *and worship* of Christ as this Church has received them."[61] Thus, the texts of the prayer book and other authorized resources are the foundation for the liturgy of The Episcopal Church. Their content and order reveal the liturgical theology of The Episcopal Church, as discussed above.

However, liturgy is not found in texts alone. Liturgy is an event. As Kevin Irwin poignantly articulates, "Each and every time we engage in the sacred liturgy, it is always a *new event*—a new event of *salvation, redemption*, and *reconciliation* with God and one another (among many other things), a new event of our *communal growth in holiness* and of our *communal self-transcendence*."[62] This event character of the liturgy is important to understand because it explains how it is theological. If liturgy is merely a series of prayers that we say in a prescribed order and, perhaps, with prescribed texts, then using liturgy as a theological source could feel legalistic. We must say the words given to us in the order given because those are the rules, and good Christians, including clergy, follow the rules. However, the liturgy is about much more than rules. It is an event leading to an encounter with the Holy One.

In the latter part of the twentieth century, liturgical scholars have emphasized liturgy's importance as *theologia prima*.[63] Rather than simply stressing the history of liturgy and correct rubrical adherence, these liturgical scholars argue that the liturgy *is* theological. They suggest that liturgy is not just an expression of theology already

---

61. 1979BCP, 526, emphasis added.

62. Irwin, *Context and Text*, xv, emphasis in original.

63. See Fagerburg, *Theologia Prima*; Irwin, *Context and Text*; Kavanagh, *On Liturgical Theology*; Lathrop, *Holy Things*; Schmemann, *Introduction to Liturgical Theology*; Taft, *Beyond East and West*.

constructed but, more profoundly, it contributes to the actual construction of theology. They often use the Latin phrase *lex orandi, lex credendi* to codify this belief.[64]

The meaning of this phrase is not self-evident, however. A literal translation is "The law of prayer [is] the law of belief." Yet greater complexity lies within it. David Fagerburg argues that "liturgical theology materializes upon the encounter with the Holy One, not upon the secondary analysis at the desk. God shapes the community in liturgical encounter, and the community makes theological adjustment to this encounter, which settles into ritual form."[65] According to Fagerburg, one's first encounter with the Holy One occurs within the liturgical experience. He is not suggesting that individuals can only experience the Holy One through liturgy and not through personal experiences outside of it. Rather, he argues that, as the Church corporately gathered, its primary experience with God is in the liturgy. This experience he calls *theologia prima*.

In turn, this encounter with God has profound effects on the Church. As the Church reflects on those profound effects, it engages in *theologia secunda*. Much of what people call theology today is *theologia secunda*. Liturgical theologians argue that the primary experience of the Holy One in the liturgy, *theologia prima*, causes the secondary reflection, *theologia secunda*.

Geoffrey Wainwright disagrees. He believes that *lex orandi, lex credendi* are interchangeable, not only in literal translation but also in the history of the Church. Wainwright argues that the history of the Church is replete with examples of how liturgy changes to meet the theological needs of the community rather than vice versa.

---

64. This phrase originates with Prosper of Aquitaine in the fifth century. See Wainwright, *Doxology*, 224-228.

65. Fagerburg, *Theologia Prima*, 9.

He provides the Reformations as an example: "Yet it was the policy of the Reformers to establish doctrinal control over worship, and the critical primacy of doctrine in relation to liturgy has remained characteristic of Protestantism."[66] Even Aidan Kavanaugh, who critiques Wainwright's position, recognizes that for the first time, an ecclesiastical authority established a particular rite as the law of the land with the English Act of Uniformity in 1549. Kavanaugh describes this as a movement toward *orthopistis* (right belief) and *orthodidascalia* (right teaching) and away from *orthodoxia* (right glory or worship).[67] The Roman Catholic Church followed suit in the Council of Trent.

However, Kavanaugh argues that the patristic maxim *legem credendi lex statuat supplicandi* ("let the law of prayer establish the law of belief") provides a more precise meaning for liturgical theology than the interchangeable *lex orandi, lex credendi*. Kavanaugh stresses that the predicate *statuat* is crucial in understanding how liturgy shapes belief in the Church. He notes that the practice of baptism led to the establishment of the Creeds, and the practice of the Eucharist led to its written accounts in Scripture rather than vice versa. For example, chapter two described how the practice of infant baptism in the Church led to Augustine's theology of original sin as a means of explaining that practice. Thus, Kavanaugh sees a direct causal relationship from the worship of the Church to the beliefs of the Church.

Is Kavanaugh correct on this point, particularly considering the history of The Episcopal Church and the BCP? Recognizing that the English Act of Uniformity in 1549 shaped the liturgy of the BCP, which can still be seen in present-day revisions, can Episcopalians

---

66. Wainwright, *Doxology*, 219.

67. Kavanaugh, *On Liturgical Theology*, 81-82.

describe themselves as a *lex orandi, lex credendi* church? Yes, they can but with qualification.

Leonel Mitchell is correct that "probably more than any other contemporary religious group, Episcopalians are people of a prayer book."[68] Without an Augsburg or Westminster Confession, Episcopalians look to the BCP as the source of their theology. Indeed, they live out this theology in their daily and weekly worship. However, Episcopalians must also recognize that the controversies of the Reformation shaped their liturgy. They cannot claim a "pure" liturgy from the early church. While their liturgy certainly has strong roots grounded in the early church, it also reflects the changes that have shaped its history since that time.

Perhaps those historical changes reflected most poignantly in the Reformations were the result of the worship experiences of the faithful during that time. For example, the emphasis on transubstantiation and clericalism as the result of eucharistic realism during the medieval period led to the desire for reform. The conclusion is a chicken-and-egg argument, which cannot prove conclusively that liturgy creates doctrine or that doctrine creates liturgy.

Since liturgy is an event and liturgical texts have been influenced by theological shifts, could we not argue that communion without baptism is such a theological shift and warrants this change? Indeed, Edmonson and other proponents of communion without baptism make this argument. Edmonson further suggests that the localized experience of worshippers is *theologia prima* and, therefore, ought to take primacy over the traditional Ordo of the Church.[69]

Edmonson and other proponents of communion without baptism argue against baptism as a demarcation between the "pure" and the

---

68. Mitchell, *Praying Shapes Believing*, 1.
69. Edmonson, *Liturgical Theology Revisited*, 3–9.

"impure."[70] They are correct in critiquing baptism as solely a purity rite. Baptism includes much greater imagery than just purification by water. As discussed in chapter two, the rich ecclesiological imagery of baptism and the Eucharist in the early Church disintegrated into flat images of exorcism for original sin and eucharistic realism in the late medieval and reformation periods.

However, Edmonson's methodology furthers the disintegration of these initiatory rites rather than supports their reunification. In his methodology, these rites remain separate units that may be switched and swapped in response to theological shifts. These shifts in the Ordo may respond to one theological issue but create many other issues. For example, the initial disintegration of the rites sought to respond to the desire for *quam primum* baptism, but created further theological problems with confirmation. As discussed above, the desire to swap communion for baptism also creates more theological challenges than it seeks to solve.

Rather than attempting to disintegrate the connection between baptism and the Eucharist even further by moving communion before baptism, the Church ought to explicitly support the indissoluble bond between baptism, the Eucharist, and the Church by placing a greater emphasis on teaching and celebrating the full and rich imagery of baptism. In their laudable desire to critique baptism as a rite for the pure, proponents of communion without baptism continue to emphasize, perhaps unwittingly, that interpretation as the primary theology for baptism, albeit in their desire to reject it. A more fruitful approach would emphasize the unitive rites with their expansive ecclesiological symbolism.

The Episcopal Church participates in the *lex orandi, lex credendi* tradition, but primarily through its use of the BCP and other

---

70. Edmonson, *Liturgical Theology Revisited*, 218-219.

authorized resources. While The Episcopal Church finds its theology within its liturgical life, it must also recognize the impact that doctrine has had on that life, as seen through the various revisions of the BCP. Therefore, a responsible liturgical theological methodology that first considers the Ordo, then the history of liturgical units, and finally, the power of juxtaposition reveals the inherent baptismal-eucharistic liturgical theology of The Episcopal Church. The next chapter discusses The Episcopal Church's baptismal-eucharistic ecclesiology.

CHAPTER FOUR

BAPTISM AND THE EUCHARIST MAKE THE CHURCH

A Baptismal-Eucharistic Ecclesiology

In chapter three, we looked closely at the baptismal-eucharistic liturgical theology of the 1979 BCP. Baptism and the Eucharist form the heart of the liturgy of The Episcopal Church as expressed in its most recent prayer book revision and, therefore, have strong implications for its ecclesiology. In this chapter, we will discuss ecclesiology from a systematic theological perspective. We will consider four ecclesiological models: a national or universal ecclesiology, an episcopal succession ecclesiology, a eucharistic ecclesiology, and a baptismal ecclesiology. We will examine the strengths and challenges of each of these models. Then, we will conclude by suggesting an alternative model: an explicit baptismal-eucharistic ecclesiology. We will argue that this alternative model provides the most robust ecclesiological expression for The Episcopal Church.

Ecclesiology is the doctrine of the Church. This branch of theology seeks to answer questions about how the Church views itself in light of Scripture, Tradition, its mission, its identification of and care for its members, the surrounding culture, and many other aspects. Paul Avis provides a helpful definition of ecclesiology as "reasoned and informed reflection on the nature of the Christian

Church."[1] Ecclesiology includes additional sub-disciplines such as missiology, pastoral theology, sacramental theology, and ecumenical theology. Fundamental theological topics such as the Trinity, Christology, and pneumatology also intersect with ecclesiology. Thus, ecclesiology touches upon all aspects of the Christian faith in some way.

However, defining an Anglican ecclesiology can be difficult. Avis correctly asserts: "There has been no single dominant Anglican ecclesiology."[2] Theologians and historians have even disputed the genesis of the Anglican Church. Is it a product of the Reformations, or can it be said to have existed before that time? Legend suggests that Christianity came to the British Isles via Joseph of Arimathea.[3] More reputable sources speak of Christianity in Britain as early as 208 CE. However, the clearest documentation becomes available in the early fourth century when three British bishops attended the Council of Arles. When the Romans left in 410, the British Church continued even when the Anglo-Saxons conquered Britain in 449. The Church in Rome reestablished contact with the British Church when Pope Gregory the Great sent St. Augustine to Canterbury in 597. This connection with the Church in Rome continued until 1534, under the authority of King Henry VIII, when the English Parliament formally severed ties with the Pope and the Church in Rome.

---

1. Avis, *The Anglican Understanding of the Church*, 2.
2. Avis, *The Anglican Understanding of the Church*, 10.
3. Patterson, *A History of the Church of England*, 1-5, 219. This citation applies to all the material in this paragraph.

A National or Universal Ecclesiology

Avis provides helpful ecclesiological models for the post-Reformation Anglican Church. The first such model he calls the "Nation-as-Church Model" or the "Erastian paradigm."[4] Erastianism is the belief that the state can and should play a role in ecclesiastical government, which intertwines the Church and state. In the case of the Church of England after the Reformations, the monarch was (and still is) the "Supreme Governor" of the Church. Bishops were members of the House of Lords in Parliament, and Anglicanism was the law of the land. The state punished dissenting groups such as Roman Catholics and Protestants using measures ranging from fines to execution for heresy. The Act of Uniformity enacted first during the reign of King Edward VI in 1549, then by Queen Elizabeth I in 1559, and then by Charles II in 1662, required the use of the BCP in all parishes.

Eventually, this model began to break down as toleration for dissenting groups increased during the nineteenth century. Parliament began to admit members from dissenting groups such as Roman Catholics, Protestant Nonconformists, and non-Christians. As Parliament gained non-Anglicans in greater numbers, it began losing credibility as the lay synod of the Church of England. Finally, the Enabling Act of 1919 reorganized the Church of England into its present-day synodical form of government.[5]

Parliament failed to uphold its responsibility as the lay synod of the Church of England, and monarchs from the seventeenth to the nineteenth centuries also failed to uphold their responsibility to be the "Supreme Governor" of the Church of England. For

---

4. Avis, *The Anglican Understanding of the Church*, 15-16.
5. Avis, *The Anglican Understanding of the Church*, 18.

example, Charles I (1625-1649) and Charles II (1660-1685) began to undermine the Anglican monopoly in government by advocating for toleration measures for all dissenting groups, eventually leading to non-Anglicans having a voice and vote in Parliament. Furthermore, James II (1685-1688) was overtly Roman Catholic and eventually was forced to vacate the throne. The Calvinist Dutchman, William of Orange (1689-1702), succeeded him with George I (1714-1727), a Lutheran, following him after Queen Anne. The culmination of these monarchical failures as "Supreme Governor" of the Church of England occurred when William IV (1830-1837) gave royal assent to the Whig party in the late 1820s. With his assent, the Whig party dissolved the bishoprics and archbishoprics in Ireland.[6] Despite these challenges, the national model persists to the modern day through the "national churches" in what would become the Anglican Communion.

These "national churches" do not remain isolated, however. As Anglicanism spread, primarily through colonialism, it began to take on a form that Nicholas Afanasiev, a Russian Orthodox priest, theologian, and émigré to Paris after the Bolshevik Revolution in 1917, described as a "universal ecclesiology."[7] The principal characteristic of universal ecclesiology is the desire to gather the entire Church under one authority, typically a single person. The clearest example of universal ecclesiology is the Roman Catholic Church, with the Pope as its head. The Roman Catholic Church recognizes the one Church as consolidating the many local churches. Therefore, advocates of universal ecclesiology argue that the Church has one visible Body on earth and should have only one visible Head on earth, the Pope.[8]

---

6. Avis, *The Anglican Understanding of the Church*, 18.
7. Afanasiev, "The Church which presides in love," 58.
8. Afanasiev, "The Church which presides in love," 66.

Throughout the history of the Church, conciliarism has been an attempt to mitigate the juridical authority of the Pope. However, Afanasiev correctly recognizes that conciliarism still depends upon primacy: "The conciliar idea cannot be set up against primacy: a council does not merely exclude primacy, it actually presupposes it. The councils cannot be gathered together automatically; they must be convoked by the head of the diocese."[9] While the Anglican Church rejected papal authority in the sixteenth century, it still faced the issue of primacy, as former colonial churches gained independence from the Church of England. These former colonial churches, including The Episcopal Church, did not wish to remain under the juridical authority of the Archbishop of Canterbury but did wish to retain a close, almost familial connection. Eventually, this desire for ecclesial connection led to the first Lambeth Conference in 1867, in which all the bishops in communion with the Church of England were invited. While the desire for such a pan-episcopal conference came from the churches, the Archbishop of Canterbury was the one to issue the invitation. Thus, conciliarity presupposes primacy.

Eventually, these many churches in communion with the See of Canterbury became known as the Anglican Communion. In 1930, the Lambeth Conference defined the Anglican Communion as

> a fellowship, within the one Holy Catholic and Apostolic Church, of those duly constituted dioceses, provinces or regional Churches in communion with the See of Canterbury, which have the following characteristics in common:
> (a) they uphold and propagate the Catholic and Apostolic faith and order as they are generally set forth in the Book of Common Prayer as authorised in their several Churches;

---

9. Afanasiev, "The Church which presides in love," 67.

(b) they are particular or national Churches, and, as such, promote within each of their territories a national expression of Christian faith, life and worship; and

(c) they are bound together not by a central legislative and executive authority, but by mutual loyalty sustained through the common counsel of the bishops in conference.[10]

While the Anglican Communion wishes to be conciliar in its structure, it grapples with the place of primacy, just as Afanasiev suggests. The Anglican Communion has developed additional structures, including the Anglican Consultative Council and the Primates Meeting, to help manage its conciliar ecclesiology. However, as the Virginia Report indicates, the See of Canterbury remains the "first among equals" and convenes the meetings of the other "Instruments of Unity," as they are called.[11] Even today, Anglicanism struggles with universal ecclesiology as it seeks to address important issues facing the Church. These issues have caused division within the Church, and many are looking for an even more centralized solution through the Anglican Covenant.

A national or universal ecclesiology provides both strengths and challenges. One of its strengths is a centralized authority that can make decisions quickly and clearly for the members within its jurisdiction. Within a national ecclesiology, that centralized authority for the Church of England was first the monarch as the Supreme Governor and then the current synodical government. In The Episcopal Church, the General Convention operates as a centralized authority, with the Executive Council acting as its representative

---

10. Coleman, ed., *Resolutions of the Twelve Lambeth Conferences 1867 – 1988*, 83-84.

11. "The Virginia Report," 19.

between sessions.[12] Internationally, the Anglican Communion has looked to the Instruments of Unity as a type of centralized authority. While they lack juridical authority, they carry a moral authority that has greater or lesser influence on member churches, often based on cultural paradigms.

National or universal ecclesiology also has its challenges. First, it lacks the robustness and dynamism necessary for contemporary ecclesiology. It relies too heavily on sterile institutionalization to support an ecclesiology that needs to be both communal and missional. Technically, the national model persists to this day in Britain, where ecclesial membership includes all persons born within the realm. However, the day-to-day support of the Church comes from the faithful few who still attend. Church attendance is at record lows. While an ecclesiological model's primary concern is theological and not logistical, it still must provide a dynamic, mission-driven model that will sustain the Church and promote the Gospel. The national model may have worked at the height of Christendom, but it will not work in today's pluralistic world.

Similarly, a national or universal ecclesiology also fails to respond to the localized needs of the Church. In its attempts to provide that universal point of view, this ecclesiology can often produce overarching pronouncements that hinder the Church's ability to respond to mission imperatives in localized contexts. Depending on the cultural paradigm, local churches may or may not follow these universal pronouncements. This variation in response to these centralized authorities often causes confusion and even resentment among the member churches. Therefore, a nimbler ecclesiological model is necessary.

---

12. "General Convention/Executive Council," The Episcopal Church, accessed May 2, 2024, http://episcopalchurch.org/page/general-convention-executive-council.

An Episcopal Succession Ecclesiology

In the nineteenth century, the Oxford Movement attempted to usher in Avis's second ecclesiological model, "the Episcopal Succession Model" or "apostolic paradigm."[13] When theologians such as John Henry Newman and John Keble, later called "the Oxford dons," heard about the dissolution of the Irish bishoprics and archbishoprics by the ruling Whig party, they grew concerned. Theological trends during this time suggested that the Church was a society with no eternal purpose. The "Oxford dons" responded with a series of pamphlets called the *Tracts for the Times*, which led to their moniker—the Tractarians.

The Tractarians responded to this ecclesiological anemia by attempting to fortify it through the episcopacy. They believed that apostolic succession—the theory that present-day bishops can trace their lineage back to the apostles through a series of laying-on-of-hands—would provide the needed ecclesiological rigor to sustain the Church. In this way, the bishop became the "sacred symbol" of the Church rather than the sovereign. The Tractarians called bishops to "Magnify your office!"—even suggesting they risk martyrdom. Comfortably institutionalized bishops, however, did not appreciate these dramatic calls to action.[14]

The Episcopal succession ecclesiology continues today, particularly in The Episcopal Church's ecumenical conversations. Because this ecclesiology provides a visible sign of unity through the office of the bishop, it often forms the framework for conversations with other churches regarding unity. For example, the Episcopal-Lutheran full communion agreement, "Called to Common Mission," speaks extensively about the importance of the episcopacy as a common bond

---

13. Avis, *The Anglican Understanding of the Church*, 19-20.
14. Avis, *The Anglican Understanding of the Church*, 20-21.

between the two churches.[15] Without a common monarch to unite these churches, the episcopacy has often become a symbol of unity.

However, Avis offers several important suggestions for the failure of this ecclesiological model. First, this model only considers the Church's apostolicity, not its catholicity. It focuses solely on the apostolic credentials of Anglican bishops and not on reestablishing communion with other Christian groups who may not have those apostolic credentials.

Second, this model does not promote ecumenical cooperation. For example, the Tractarians believed apostolic succession would be enough to reestablish communion with Rome. However, because Roman Catholic bishops are only recognized within the context of their hierarchical communion *vis-à-vis* the Pope, they will not recognize Anglican bishops despite their apostolic credentials.[16] This model also fails because it attempts to make the episcopate essential to the Church's existence. Thus, it would excommunicate entire swaths of the Church that are not episcopally structured. Avis points out that current ecumenical theology sees apostolicity through the broader lens of faithful apostolic ministry, regardless of order.[17]

Lastly, this model fails to recognize the need for a robust ecclesiological model to address the modern world's pluralistic concerns. While the episcopate remains an important sign of unity for the Church, Avis is correct that this model places too much weight on it. If the Church believes that soteriology and ecclesiology are dynamically interrelated, then an ecclesiological model that

---

15. *Called to Common Mission*, 6-10.

16. Pope Leo XIII declared in *Apostolicae Curae* in 1896: "We pronounce and declare that Ordinations carried out according to the Anglican rite have been and are absolutely null and utterly void." Found in "The English Text of *Apostolicae Curae*," in Franklin, ed., *Anglican Orders*, 136.

17. Avis, *The Anglican Understanding of the Church*, 22-23.

excommunicates large portions of the Church is insufficient and theologically reckless. Furthermore, this model promotes the episcopacy so strongly that it almost negates the other orders of ministry, both lay and ordained. The Church needs a model that promotes the ministries of all its members.

A Eucharistic Ecclesiology

The early twentieth century brought with it changes in ecclesiology. Ecclesiologies based on national, universal, and episcopal succession models did not provide robust theological alternatives. In his essay, "The Church which presides in love," Afanasiev argues for a different ecclesiology: a eucharistic ecclesiology. Rather than viewing the Church as one body spread out over the earth with one visible head, the Pope, a eucharistic ecclesiology sees the local Church as the fullness of the Church.

> Every local church enjoys all the fullness of the Church of God in Christ. The plurality of local churches does not destroy the unity of the Church of God, just as the plurality of eucharistic assemblies does not destroy the unity of the Eucharist in time and space.... And so eucharistic ecclesiology in no way rejects the universality of the Church but makes a distinction between exterior universality (in so far as the mission is limited), and interior universality which equals itself always and in all circumstances, because it means that the Church manifests itself everywhere, always in fullness and unity.[18]

Thus, the Eucharist becomes the unifying ecclesiological principle rather than a supreme pontiff. The presider of the Eucharist is the

---

18. Afanasiev, "The Church which presides in love," 76.

visible sign of unity for the assembly. However, the presider can only preside when the assembly gathers. Therefore, the presider is not over the assembly but in the midst of it.[19]

Roman Catholic, Anglican, and Orthodox theologians have supported Afanasiev's profound connection between the Eucharist and the Church. For example, Henri de Lubac, known for his influence on the Second Vatican Council, stated, "The Eucharist makes the Church."[20] The Church expresses its most profound unity through the Eucharist, in which Christ, as Head of the Church, joins with his Body. In a 2001 paper entitled, "The Eucharist: Sacrament of unity," the Church of England's House of Bishops builds on de Lubac's fundamental statement: "The Eucharist stands at the very heart of the life, worship and mission of the Christian Church."[21] However, de Lubac considers eucharistic ecclesiology too limiting in its description of the structure of the Church. While he certainly supports the central role that the Eucharist plays in ecclesiology, he is not ready to support a specifically eucharistic ecclesiology. He believes that a complete ecclesiology must be broader than just the Eucharist to address the needs of mission.[22]

Orthodox theologian John Zizioulas also critiques Afanasiev's eucharistic ecclesiology. Zizioulas believes the bishop must play a much more central role in ecclesiology. Afanasiev recognizes the bishop as the primary presider of the Eucharist but finds the locus of episcopal authority within the assembly itself.[23] Zizioulas, on the other hand, considers the bishop to be the locus of unity in the Church, who is

---

19. Afanasiev, "The Church which presides in love," 77-80.
20. As quoted in McPartlan, *The Eucharist Makes the Church*, xv.
21. *The Eucharist: Sacrament of Unity*, vii.
22. McPartlan, *The Eucharist Makes the Church*, 98.
23. Afanasiev, "The Church which presides in love," 108.

then able to call the assembly together: "When the historian looks at the Eucharist as the supreme incorporation of the Church in Christ in space and time, this necessarily leads to an examination also of the bishop as the center of unity in each Church."[24] Zizioulas does not consider the parish with the presbyter as presider to be the locus of unity for the Church but rather the diocese with the bishop as the primary presider: "the concept of the local Church is guaranteed *by the bishop* and not by the presbyter: the local Church as an entity with full ecclesiological status is the *episcopal diocese* and not the parish."[25] Zizioulas argues that the ancient Church saw the bishop as the central authority, with the presbyters gathered around the bishop as the disciples gathered around Christ. Just as Christ stands in as the one for the many in his crucifixion, the bishop also stands in as the one for the many in the anamnesis of Christ's crucifixion in the Eucharist. According to Zizioulas, without the bishop, the Church does not exist. He almost appears to be advocating for an "Episcopal succession" ecclesiology. However, Zizioulas strongly connects the bishop with the Eucharist so much that Episcopal succession alone is insufficient for him.

While Zizioulas critiques Afanasiev's focus on the parish as the local church, he also expands significantly on the ontological importance of the Eucharist in terms of personhood, illuminating a significant strength of eucharistic ecclesiology. His seminal work *Being as Communion* develops his theology of personhood. A full development of this theology lies outside the scope of this work. Briefly, Zizioulas argues that the fundamental nature of the Trinity is *koinonia* or communion. Through baptism, a person is reborn into the life of the Trinity and becomes an "ecclesial hypostasis."[26]

---

24. Zizioulas, *Eucharist, Bishop, Church*, 18.
25. Zizioulas, *Being as Communion*, 251.
26. Zizioulas, *Being as Communion*, 53.

Because the Orthodox Church recognizes the inherent unity of baptism, chrismation, and the Eucharist in a single ritual event, the newly baptized immediately enters the eucharistic community. The newly baptized is no longer an individual but becomes a true person, a "sacramental or eucharistic hypostasis."[27] Therefore, the Eucharist is not simply a gathering of individuals who desire to express common beliefs. Instead, the Eucharist draws each person up into the life of God, not as individuals, but as the Body of Christ. Thus, an existential change transforms each individual into a true person. For Zizioulas, the Eucharist not only makes the Church but also makes the person.

An additional strength of eucharistic ecclesiology is that it recognizes the locus of the Church in the eucharistic assembly. For Afanasiev, the bishop is the primary presider of that eucharistic assembly but only through the assembly itself. For Zizioulas, the bishop convenes the eucharistic assembly. Without the bishop, the Eucharist does not exist. Similarly, without the Eucharist, the bishop does not exist. Therefore, as de Lubac suggests, "The Eucharist makes the Church."

However, one of the major critiques of eucharistic ecclesiology is its tendency toward triumphalism. Because eucharistic ecclesiology focuses on the local assembly, it can become insular and eventually triumphalist. As Erickson points out, "Needed today are structures for communion, common activity and witness that transcend the dichotomy of 'local' and 'universal.'"[28] In a world that is rapidly shrinking due to globalization and instantaneous communication, the Church cannot succumb to the temptation toward insularity or triumphalism. The Church must continue to strive for greater

---

27. Zizioulas, *Being as Communion*, 59.

28. Erickson, "The Church in modern Orthodox thought: towards a baptismal ecclesiology," 2-3, 145.

cooperation and greater understanding. The Church needs an ecclesiology that recognizes its common identity in Christ rather than focusing on its differences.

Another critique of eucharistic ecclesiology is its intermittency. Zizioulas makes important contributions to not only ecclesiology but theological anthropology with his doctrine of the "sacramental or eucharistic hypostasis." However, he fails to explain how this new hypostatic existence persists outside of the eucharistic assembly. This eucharistically hypostatic existence has an intermittent quality to it that McPartlan pointedly describes.

> For Zizioulas, what we are as Christians is what we are, strictly speaking, only in momentary, eucharistic events in this world; but these events are *ontologically definitive*. The Christian lives in them and out of them.[29]

While Zizioulas' doctrine of eucharistic hypostasis has already had profound effects on Christian theology, it needs further development. An intermittent identity cannot sustain the Church. To accomplish Christ's mission in the world, members of the Church need an ecclesial identity that persists beyond the eucharistic assembly.

A Baptismal Ecclesiology

Along with a eucharistic ecclesiology, the twentieth century also saw the development of a baptismal ecclesiology. Ruth Meyers, in her comprehensive work *Continuing the Reformation*, describes in great detail the process by which The Episcopal Church adopted a baptismal ecclesiology with the revision of its most recent prayer

---

29. McPartlan, *The Eucharist Makes the Church*, 273-274.

book.³⁰ She concludes her work by naming specific ways in which this ecclesiology has permeated the institutional structures of The Episcopal Church through the Executive Council, the Standing Commission on the Structure of the Church, various surveys, and the fundamental role that the baptismal covenant has played in the ordination of women.³¹ For example, the baptismal covenant has become a centerpiece of the ecclesiology of The Episcopal Church.

In his book *An Introduction to World Anglicanism*, Kaye describes The Episcopal Church as being "framed within a concept of baptismal covenant. The church was the community of the baptised and a baptismal covenant provided the context for all that the church was to do and be."³² Much of The Episcopal Church's missiology stems from the baptismal covenant. Thus, The Episcopal Church adopted a baptismal ecclesiology through its most recent prayer book revision. This baptismal ecclesiology's strengths include implications for identity and ecumenism.

A baptismal ecclesiology begins with a readjusted view of ecclesial identity. In a baptismal ecclesiology, all baptized members of the Church are ordained ministers of the Church. As Kavanaugh so aptly states,

> While every presbyter and bishop is therefore a sacerdotal person, not every sacerdotal person in the Church is a presbyter or bishop. Nor does sacerdotality come upon one for the first time, so to speak, at one's ordination. In constant genesis in the font, the Church is born there as a sacerdotal assembly by the Spirit of the anointed One himself. *Laos* is a priestly name for a priestly person.³³

---

30. As outlined in chapter two.
31. Meyers, *Continuing the Reformation*, 227-237.
32. Kaye, *An Introduction to World Anglicanism*, 225.
33. Kavanagh, "Unfinished and Unbegun Revisited," 269.

As described in chapter two, many of the ancient baptismal rites included imagery of ordination, such as a stole being given to the newly baptized. The newly baptized were considered full ministers of the Church.

A baptismal ecclesiology does not recognize an ontological difference between the laity and the clergy. Each is a charismatic minister of the Church. While Afanasiev popularized a eucharistic ecclesiology, he firmly believed in baptism as an ordination rite. He coined the term "laic" instead of a layperson to signify the connection between the orders: "One cannot be in the Church and not be a laic, *laikos*—a member of God's people. Everyone in the Church is a laic and all together are God's people and each one is called, as a priest of God, to offer spiritual sacrifices to Him through Jesus Christ."[34]

Later in the medieval Church, the priest alone became the one who offered spiritual sacrifice as the role of the laity diminished. However, such a view distorts the true calling of all baptized persons as "laics" in the Church. Zizioulas agrees with Afanasiev regarding baptism as ordination:

> The conclusion is that ordination is *a primordial and constitutive act of the Christian community*. This primordial character of ordination is to be seen in the fact that there is actually no such person as a 'non-ordained' member of the Church. It is a mistake to call the lay members of the Church 'non-ordained'. Baptism and especially confirmation (chrismation) as an inseparable aspect of the rite of initiation involves a 'laying on of hands' and a 'seal' (*sphragis*), and *inevitably and immediately* leads the baptized person to the eucharistic community in

---

34. Afanasiev, *The Church of the Holy Spirit*, 10.

order to assume his particular '*ordo*' there. The laity do not represent either a morally lower or a generically general and 'prior' kind of charismatic existence, but exist *together with* the other orders.[35]

These strong proponents of eucharistic ecclesiology see baptism as the constitutive event for such an ecclesiology. Through baptism, individuals within the assembly identify themselves with Christ, who draws them into the inner life of the Trinity. No other ordination can perform a more profound act than baptism. Baptism truly reorients one's entire identity.

This reoriented identity has practical implications for ecclesiology as well. For example, groups within The Episcopal Church use this baptismal identity to support progressive positions within the Church. When asked why he supported the ordination of women, Bishop Morris based his answer on baptism:

> In Baptism, women, like men, are made members of Christ, children of God, and inheritors of the Kingdom of Heaven. They are, therefore, unless the Church's custom of baptizing women is erroneous, capable of sharing in the identity of Christ, and, in the lay role, of representing him. If this is true, there is no ground whatever for supposing that women are intrinsically incapable of entering into the role of the person who sacramentally represents to the Church its identity in Christ. Indeed, it seems that to make this assertion would be implicitly to deny or to qualify the meaning of women's baptisms.[36]

---

35. Zizioulas, "Ordination—A Sacrament? An Orthodox Reply," 36.

36. Morris, Fairweather, Griffiss and Mollegen, "A Report on The Validity of the Philadelphia Ordinations," 188.

Thus, Bishop Morris draws an explicit connection between a woman's baptism and her ability to be ordained. In essence, Bishop Morris recognizes that women are already ordained members of the Church by their baptism. Ordination as presbyters recognizes their gifts to preside at the Eucharist.

Louis Weil also draws on baptism as the key reason for not only the ordination of women but also the ordination of homosexual persons:

> If discernment concerning suitability for holy orders is grounded in a baptismal ecclesiology, then the fundamental issue is not a person's gender or sexual orientation, but rather the evidence of the charisms that the church needs in its ordained leaders.[37]

Both Weil and Morris recognize baptism as the true ordination for ministry in the Church. They would argue that subsequent ordination to the priesthood presupposes this prior ordination and does not depend upon any inherent characteristics within the person. Instead, it builds on the charisms the Holy Spirit gives in baptism/chrismation.

This baptismal ecclesiology has permeated The Episcopal Church, and some of the current debates within the Anglican Communion stem from a misunderstanding of its view of baptismal identity. Other churches within the Anglican Communion misunderstand the importance that The Episcopal Church places upon baptismal identity. As Kaye suggests,

> Such a presentation of the situation means that in the present debates, when gay and lesbian people are said to be members of the church, this has a much more significant connotation

---

37. Weil, "Baptismal Ecclesiology: Uncovering a Paradigm," 26.

in ECUSA than in other parts of the Anglican Communion, where membership is less precisely defined and more loosely conceived and where the democratic spirit is not so rigorously in place."[38]

The intention here is not to debate the theological merits of the ordination of women or homosexual persons but rather to draw attention to baptism as the fundamental argument in favor of such ordinations. The baptismal ecclesiology of The Episcopal Church has had a profound effect on the identity of its members as ministers of the Church.

An additional strength of this ecclesiology is its implications for ecumenism. Avis reminds us that "Anglicans hold that the unity of the Church is grounded in the one baptism. They have been among the first to perceive the ecumenical significance of the mutual recognition of baptism by the churches."[39] Anglicans believe baptism provides for the fundamental unity of the Church of Christ. As early as 1920, the Lambeth Conference recognized, "We acknowledge all those who believe in our Lord Jesus Christ, and have been baptized into the name of the Holy Trinity, as sharing with us membership in the universal Church of Christ which is his Body."[40] Thus, baptism became the unifying event in The Episcopal Church's ecumenical relationships with other Christian churches. In chapter five, we will explore the ecumenical significance of baptism and the Eucharist more thoroughly.

However, we want to draw attention to the way in which a baptismal ecclesiology distinguishes itself from a eucharistic

---

38. Kaye, *An Introduction to World Anglicanism*, 227.
39. Avis, *The Anglican Understanding of the Church*, 74.
40. Coleman, *Resolutions of the Twelve Lambeth Conferences 1867–1988*, 45-46.

ecclesiology through its implications for ecumenism. While Zizioulas recognizes the Eucharist as the constitutive event of the Church and baptism as the ordination of all members within the eucharistic community, he still sees differences in orthodoxy as a barrier to full communion among the churches:

> Judged from this viewpoint, any attempt at 'intercommunion' between Churches divided by heresy or schism is unthinkable according to the sources of the period examined here. Communion in the eucharist presupposes full unity in all the basics, such as love and faith ('let us love one another, that with one mind we may confess...'), because eucharistic unity constitutes the culmination and full expression of the unity of the Church.[41]

One must then wonder if the Eucharist is truly the source of unity within the Church for Zizioulas or if agreement on orthodoxy prevails.

Erickson critiques Zizioulas on this very count. He believes that a purely eucharistic ecclesiology, particularly as articulated in the Orthodox Church, focuses too strongly on the local eucharistic assembly. This focus can lead to an insularism that becomes triumphalism:

> By failing to see the Eucharist in the light of baptism, eucharistic ecclesiology too easily lends itself to triumphalism.... Along with triumphalism, eucharistic ecclesiology too easily lends itself to what has been called 'ecclesiological and soteriological exclusivism.'[42]

---

41. Zizioulas, *Eucharist, Bishop, Church*, 258.

42. Erickson, "The Church in modern Orthodox thought: towards a baptismal ecclesiology," 149.

Baptismal ecclesiology attempts to mitigate this "ecclesiological and soteriological exclusivism" by recognizing the Church's inherent unity in baptism.

Therefore, Anglicans support full communion within the Church by each member's common baptism. Avis recognizes the importance of baptism for Anglicans as the foundation for full communion with other churches:

> By their practice of eucharistic hospitality, Anglicans show that they believe that the common baptism calls for unity in the eucharist—for that is where the body of Christ, to which we already belong by baptism, is most fully known. The eucharist, or holy communion, is the paradigm of *koinonia* and this concept—so fruitful in current ecumenical work—is particularly congenial to Anglicans.[43]

Baptism provides the necessary communion through which the Eucharist can be celebrated. The Church's identification with Christ through baptism, not through a common understanding of orthodoxy, allows for full communion. Christ draws each person to himself through the waters of baptism, in the anointing of the Holy Spirit, and finally into the eucharistic assembly. Baptism, not orthodoxy, draws everyone into the One Body of Christ.

Therefore, baptismal ecclesiology holds much merit. It profoundly reorients one's identity toward Christ. This new ecclesial identity is one's first ordination into ministry. Any subsequent ordination presupposes one's primary ordination through baptism. Additionally, baptismal ecclesiology provides a common identity that allows for greater ecumenical cooperation and eventual full communion among the churches.

---

43. Avis, *The Anglican Understanding of the Church*, 74.

However, baptismal ecclesiology also provides challenges. Paul Gibson raises questions about the extent to which a baptismal ecclesiology can support the church's structures. While affirming the egalitarian spirit of baptismal ecclesiology, he recognizes baptism as "the door; the table is where structure and order are defined."[44] He supports a eucharistic ecclesiology, as the Church finds the necessary order to conduct its affairs in the structure of the Eucharist.

Like Gibson, Lizette Larson-Miller raises concerns about the failure of a baptismal ecclesiology to make an explicit connection between baptism, chrismation, and the Eucharist. She poignantly asks, "What does it mean to say that Eucharist is no longer the completion of initiation, or that there is no validity to chrismation?"[45] By making baptism "full initiation" into the Church, did the 1979 BCP inadvertently sever the essential connection between baptism, chrismation, and the Eucharist as a unitive rite? Larson-Miller makes this very point as she discusses the practice of communion without baptism. Larson-Miller astutely notes, "This conversation surrounding the prayer book may very well be the source of the inadvertent shift to initiation without eucharistic summation. Of the many questions that this shift raises, the first, 'How did we get to a place where we blithely espouse a baptimsal ecclesiology without baptism?' in turn raises the possibility that the formative conversation may have been so focused on the immediate polemics that it missed other important threads."[46] Larson-Miller questions whether a baptismal ecclesiology is fulsome enough to support the entirety of a Christian's sacramental encounter with Christ without an explicit reference to initiation's summation in the Eucharist. She encourages further exploration of communion

---

44. Gibson, "A Baptismal Ecclesiology – Some Questions," 44.
45. Larson-Miller, *Sacramentality Renewed*, 141.
46. Larson-Miller, *Sacramentality Renewed*, 141-142.

ecclesiologies and Eucharistic ecclesiologies in better understanding the sacramentality of the Church.

In her essay "Baptismal Ecclesiology without Baptism?" Larson-Miller also raises concerns about a baptismal ecclesiology that does not mention communion.[47] Situating the conversation in the postmodern milieu, she voices concerns about the contemporary obsession with the individual, "If the church, the body of Christ, is 'we together' and our cultural practices prevent us from recognizing anything real about 'we,' what are we to do beyond functioning as another club, support group, or comfortable affinity group, acting in order to reconfirm one's own centrality in all reality?"[48]

Thus, baptismal ecclesiology can lead to a theology of "rights" in which members of the Church believe they have a "right" to aspects of ecclesial life by their baptism. When this expectation of certain rights, for example to ordination, occurs, then the focus of baptism incorrectly shifts to the individual rather than remaining in the community. This individualistic identity cannot sustain the Church. Therefore, baptismal ecclesiology's focus on identity can develop into greater separation if it does not lead immediately to the eucharistic community. Baptism identifies each person with Christ, the Crucified-Risen One. Christ came "to seek out and to save the lost" (Luke 19:10), not to establish rights. Through baptism, each person identifies with Christ and can say with Paul, "I have been crucified with Christ; and it is no longer I who live, but it is Christ who lives in me" (Galatians 2:19-20). Through identification with Christ, one certainly seeks justice for the poor, the widowed, and the oppressed (Matthew 25:31-41), but not for oneself. The contemporary outcry for "my rights!" in much of Western society is not a Christian

---

47. Larson-Miller, "Baptismal Ecclesiology without Baptism?," 85.
48. Larson-Miller, "Baptismal Ecclesiology without Baptism?," 87.

teaching. The Church needs an ecclesiology that does not lead to greater separation from each other but rather to greater communion with each other.

A Baptismal-Eucharistic Ecclesiology: The Hyphen Really Matters

While baptismal and eucharistic ecclesiologies have much to offer The Episcopal Church, they are incomplete. In this section, we will make the case for a baptismal-eucharistic ecclesiology as the most robust ecclesiological expression for The Episcopal Church. We will provide three reasons why: clarity, wholeness, and mission. Finally, we will identify inter-Anglican agreements that support a baptismal-eucharistic ecclesiology.

A baptismal-eucharistic ecclesiology provides the most robust ecclesiology for The Episcopal Church, first through clarity. Both the proponents of a eucharistic ecclesiology and of a baptismal ecclesiology have recognized the inherent connection between baptism and the Eucharist. However, significant misunderstandings have occurred due to a lack of clarity. For example, some scholars have suggested that Zizioulas passes quickly through baptism to get to the Eucharist.[49] Yet, Zizioulas considers baptism to be a constitutive event for ecclesial hypostasis, the foundation for his doctrine of personhood.[50] Conversely, Gibson critiques Weil's baptismal ecclesiology for lacking the structural rigor that the Eucharist provides.[51] However, after understanding that Weil considers the Eucharist to be the completion

---

49. See McPartlan, *The Eucharist Makes the Church*, 273 and Erickson, "The Church in modern Orthodox thought: towards a baptismal ecclesiology," 144.

50. Zizioulas, *Being as Communion*, 53.

51. Gibson, "A Baptismal Ecclesiology – Some Questions," 44.

of the initiatory rite begun with baptism, he modifies his critique. Gibson rightly states:

> If the [International Anglican Liturgical Commission] had defined baptism as the water rite and the eucharist combined—which I believe is the proper definition of Christian Initiation—there would be no need for the rest of this paper. However, it is my sense that most readers understand baptism to mean the water rite alone. I believe an ecclesiology must have a broader and deeper base.[52]

The Church cannot rely on inherent or obscure meanings in an important area like ecclesiology. A baptismal-eucharistic ecclesiology provides clarity that avoids misunderstandings.

Furthermore, a baptismal-eucharistic ecclesiology clarifies the indissoluble bond between baptism, the Eucharist, and the Church. A baptismal-eucharistic ecclesiology recognizes that baptism precedes the Eucharist. However, unlike a "baptismal eucharistic ecclesiology" with no hyphen, the hyphen indicates the indissoluble bond between baptism and the Eucharist. Without the hyphen, a gap exists between baptism and the Eucharist that historically has extended to several years. As discussed in chapter two, this gap can develop into significant implications for ecclesiology that mitigate the identity of the laity as ministers in the Church and allow for a rise in clericalism.

A "eucharistic baptismal ecclesiology," in which the Eucharist precedes baptism with a gap of time intervening, as proponents of communion without baptism suggest, also causes ecclesiological problems. Are members fully initiated into the Church simply by receiving communion one time? As discussed in chapter three, the postcommunion prayer in the 1979 BCP explicitly thanks God for

---

52. Gibson, "A Baptismal Ecclesiology – Some Questions," 35.

making communicants "living members of your Son our Savior Jesus Christ."[53] Ecclesial identity remains unclear in this ecclesiology.

Furthermore, a "eucharistic baptismal ecclesiology" could lead to a "eucharistic ecclesiology" with baptism missing entirely. If local assemblies fail to promote the need for baptism robustly, communicants who are unbaptized could remain so indefinitely. Would baptism be required for confirmation or for ordination? The same theological arguments supporting communion without baptism could theoretically support ordination without baptism. Would baptism disappear? Edmonson argues it should not, but the possibility is more than theoretical.[54]

Finally, a "eucharistic baptismal ecclesiology" could lead to further clericalism. As discussed above, baptism results in a change of identity. One becomes a new person in Christ and, thus, shares in the eternal priesthood of Christ. As co-priests in Christ, the baptized actively participate in the Eucharist, not as spectators or mere recipients of communion but as priestly intercessors. Without that baptismal initiation into Christ, how does one actively participate with the Body of Christ in the Eucharist? Could the Eucharist be reduced again, as in the Middle Ages, to a passive spectator experience in which the ordained priests render Christ present in the Eucharist and the congregation merely receives communion? The division between the clergy and laity (if one could be called a *laic* without baptism) would grow. Therefore, a baptismal-eucharistic ecclesiology provides needed clarity about this indissoluble bond.

In addition to clarity, a baptismal-eucharistic ecclesiology provides wholeness. It understands that baptism is initiation as full members of the Church. Ordered ministry relates to charisms,

---

53. 1979BCP, 365.

54. Edmonson, *Liturgical Theology Revisited*, 85.

not to ontological changes. The anointing of the Spirit in baptism/chrismation empowers members of the Church for ministry:

> There can be no non-charismatic members in the Church, just as there can be no members who do not minister in it. The difference in gifts does not entail a difference in grace or its fullness. Grace is not distributed differentially. There is fullness of grace in each gift.[55]

A baptismal-eucharistic ecclesiology recognizes no ontological distinction between lay persons and clergy but only a distinction in gifts. Baptism calls everyone to ministry. Some members may be called to areas of ordained leadership requiring certain charisms, but that call makes no distinction between one's membership in the Body of Christ.

A baptismal-eucharistic ecclesiology provides wholeness by explicitly recognizing the community in which those gifts are to be shared—the eucharistic community. As mentioned above, while baptism changes one's identity, it does not give one "rights" within the Church. Membership in the Church is unlike membership in a social club, where certain rights and privileges are provided. Membership in the Church is incorporation into Christ, the Crucified-Risen One, as experienced most poignantly in the Eucharist. Just as Christ surrendered all his rights in his crucifixion, the baptized surrender all their rights in service to Christ.

Finally, a baptismal-eucharistic ecclesiology provides for mission. As discussed above, eucharistic ecclesiology offers an intermittent identity that only occurs when the eucharistic assembly gathers. How can it provide for the missional needs of the Church outside of that community? Matthew 28:19 instructs the Church, "Go therefore and

---

55. Afanasiev, *The Church of the Holy Spirit*, 16.

make disciples of all nations, baptizing them in the name of the Father and of the Son and of the Holy Spirit." It does not instruct the Church to "make disciples of all nations, *eucharitizing* them" but "baptizing them." Baptism is not just about one's identity within the Church but one's identity within the world.

Baptism is about mission. By being transformed through identification with Christ, the Church seeks to bring others to him so they might be transformed. However, that mission does not end with baptism. Matthew 28:20 continues, "and teaching them to obey everything that I have commanded you. And remember, I am with you always, to the end of the age." Here, the author of Matthew invokes eucharistic imagery because the Eucharist provides the context by which the Church teaches others the commandments of Christ. It is also where the Church experiences the Real Presence of Christ most profoundly. Once again, an Ordo is evident: mission-teaching-baptism-Eucharist. Thus, a baptismal-eucharistic ecclesiology is a missional ecclesiology.

Lastly, several inter-Anglican agreements support a baptismal-eucharistic ecclesiology.[56] The Chicago-Lambeth Quadrilateral is one of the earliest agreements that implicitly recognized a baptismal-eucharistic ecclesiology. It is in the Historical Documents at the back of the BCP. It accompanies other important documents such as the "Definition of the Union of the Divine and Human Natures in the Person of Christ" from the Council of Chalcedon, "The Creed of Saint Athanasius," the preface to the first 1549 BCP, and the "Articles of Religion."[57] The House of Bishops of The Episcopal Church first adopted the Chicago-Lambeth Quadrilateral in 1886. The Lambeth Conference in 1888 subsequently adopted it. It states, "That we

---

56. Chapter five discusses Anglican ecumenical dialogues.
57. *Book of Common Prayer*, 1979, 864-878.

believe that all who have been duly baptized with water, in the name of the Father, and of the Son, and of the Holy Ghost, are members of the Holy Catholic Church." It then continues:

> As inherent parts of this sacred deposit, and therefore as essential to the restoration of unity among the divided branches of Christendom, we account the following, to wit: ... The two Sacraments,—Baptism and the Supper of the Lord,—ministered with unfailing use of Christ's words of institution and of the elements ordained by Him.[58]

These statements not only recognize baptism as a principle of unity among the churches but also acknowledge its connection with the Lord's Supper or the Eucharist. Granted, this agreement also recognizes the importance of episcopacy as an area of ecumenical agreement, which would align it with the "Episcopal Succession" model that Avis described. Nonetheless, recognizing the bishop as the primary presider at baptism and the Eucharist connects it to a baptismal-eucharistic ecclesiology.

Lambeth Resolutions proceeding from this time forward portray further developments of a baptismal-eucharistic ecclesiology. For example, Lambeth Resolution 9 from 1920 continues to urge the episcopacy as a sign of unity but does so through connection with baptism and the Eucharist.[59] Resolutions 100 through 112 from the Lambeth Conference 1948 discuss the relationship between baptism and confirmation. Resolution 103 explicitly states, "the Conference considers that it is not desirable to change the present sequence of Baptism, Confirmation, and admission to Holy Communion."[60]

---

58. *Book of Common Prayer*, 1979, 876, and 877, respectively.
59. Coleman, *Resolutions of the Twelve Lambeth Conferences 1867–1988*, 45-48.
60. Coleman, *Resolutions of the Twelve Lambeth Conferences 1867–1988*, 117.

Then, in 1958, the Lambeth Conference cautioned member churches that were undergoing prayer book revision by

> call[ing] attention to those features in the Books of Common Prayer which are essential to the safeguarding of our unity: i.e. the use of the canonical Scriptures and the Creeds, Holy Baptism, Confirmation, Holy Communion, and the Ordinal.[61]

Finally, the Lambeth Conference 1968 recognized the direct link between baptism and the ministry of the laity in resolution 25: "The Conference recommends that each province or regional Church be asked to explore the theology of baptism and confirmation in relation to the need to commission the laity for their task in the world, and to experiment in this regard."[62] While Lambeth Conference resolutions are not binding on any member churches, they reveal the "mind of the Anglican Communion" at that time. These resolutions show that the Anglican Communion has historically seen a close connection between baptism, the Eucharist, and the Church.

Constitution and canons are another important inter-Anglican agreement. While the canons of The Episcopal Church are a covenant among its members, they also serve to inform other churches of the Anglican Communion, as well as ecumenical partners, about The Episcopal Church's theology and practice. In 1982, the General Convention of The Episcopal Church significantly revised the canon entitled "Of Regulations Respecting the Laity."[63] This canon, which became effective in 1985, states in section 7, "No unbaptized person shall be eligible to receive Holy Communion in this Church."[64] This

---

61. Coleman, *Resolutions of the Twelve Lambeth Conferences 1867 – 1988*, 137.
62. Coleman, *Resolutions of the Twelve Lambeth Conferences 1867 – 1988*, 161.
63. *Annotated Constitution and Canons*, 32.
64. *Constitution and Canons*, 2022, 49.

canon persists to the current edition in 2022.[65] Of course, the Church can and has changed its canons to reflect changes in its theology and practice. However, the canons not only provide a binding covenant among the members of The Episcopal Church but also serve as a theological witness for the wider Church.

"The Virginia Report," received by the Anglican Consultative Council in 1997 and the Lambeth Conference of 1998, is another important inter-Anglican agreement that recognizes an inherent baptismal-eucharistic ecclesiology. A baptismal-eucharistic ecclesiology permeates this report. Section 2.23 provides a significant example:

> To be baptized and to participate at the Table of the Lord is to be entrusted with Christ's one, continuing mission through the Church. The baptised are called to unity and interdependence. United to Christ, each member of the Body relates to the other members; they are interdependent with and through Christ. To celebrate the eucharist together reveals and builds this mutuality. "We who are many are one body for we all partake of the one bread". In eucharist the Spirit affirms and renews communion in Christ and the gifts given us to participate in the divine mission.[66]

This section of the report poignantly illuminates the ecclesiological connection between baptism, the Eucharist, unity, interdependence, mutuality, and mission within the Church. In fact, one can hardly imagine the Church without this interdependence of baptism and the Eucharist. "The Virginia Report" vividly describes a baptismal-eucharistic ecclesiology.

---

65. *Constitution and Canons*, 2009, Title 1 Canon 17.7.
66. "The Virginia Report," 14.

Finally, in 2009, the Theology Committee of the House of Bishops addressed the issue of the relationship between baptism and the Eucharist directly, in a paper entitled "Reflections on Holy Baptism and the Holy Eucharist." In this paper, they attempt to speak to the issue of "open communion" or communion without baptism. In doing so, they list several important images regarding the relationship of baptism and the Eucharist:

- Baptism unites one to Christ. One receives thereby Christ's own Spirit as the power to lead a reformed, Christ-like life. In the eucharist one actually draws upon that life-giving Spirit, which comes to us through the gift of Christ's own humanity to us in the elements, to grow into and sustain under trial a Christ-like transformation of life.
- Baptism inaugurates a particular relationship into which one then lives empowered and renewed through the eucharist. In baptism one is graciously adopted into God's household and then nourished by God. Believers receive the Spirit in baptism leading to sanctification by the Spirit's work in the eucharist.
- Our baptism is a baptism into the death and resurrection of Christ. We recognize with Paul that our eucharistic practice proclaims the Lord's death until he comes.
- In baptism one is made a member of Christ. In the eucharist we both remember and are remembered as the body of Christ.
- In baptism we are cleansed from sin and raised to newness of life. In the eucharist we partake of the blood of Christ which was shed for the forgiveness of our sins.[67]

---

67. Theology Committee of the House of Bishops of the Episcopal Church, "Reflection on Holy Baptism and the Holy Eucharist," 146.

These images intricately connect baptism with the Eucharist. The first image shows one's connection to Christ first through baptism and then on an ongoing basis through the Eucharist. The second image speaks of one's relationship with God being "inaugurated" through baptism and then "nourished" in the Eucharist. Baptism also involves identification with Christ's death and resurrection, and then the Eucharist continually proclaims that central tenet of one's faith. Baptism makes someone a member, and the Eucharist "remembers" that person. Finally, baptism cleanses one from sin, and the Eucharist provides ongoing forgiveness of sins through partaking in Christ's blood. The theology committee concludes this section: "All of these ways presume that baptism leads to eucharist and not the other way around."[68]

In addition, the committee reflects on how these images permeate both the historic liturgies of the Church as well as The Episcopal Church's current prayer book theology. They also respond to the suggestion that Jesus' table fellowship permits "open communion" by recollecting that Jesus nearly always ate with fellow Jews, who were also in a covenant relationship with God. Additionally, he was rarely ever the host extending an invitation but rather the guest accepting an invitation.[69] Therefore, the committee concludes, "It is essential to understand the doctrinal and liturgical connections between baptism and eucharist, especially in a church that has been affirming the centrality of baptism."[70] While not explicit, this conclusion strongly implies a baptismal-eucharistic ecclesiology. With these considerations, The Episcopal Church should make a more explicit

---

68. Theology Committee of the House of Bishops of the Episcopal Church, "Reflection on Holy Baptism and the Holy Eucharist," 147.

69. Theology Committee of the House of Bishops of the Episcopal Church, "Reflection on Holy Baptism and the Holy Eucharist," 147.

70. Theology Committee of the House of Bishops of the Episcopal Church, "Reflection on Holy Baptism and the Holy Eucharist," 151.

statement supporting the indissoluble bond between baptism, the Eucharist, and the Church.

Anglicanism has long struggled to identify its ecclesiology. After the Reformations, the Church of England adopted a national ecclesiology that has now become a universal ecclesiology by virtue of the Instruments of Unity. This universal ecclesiology provides for centralized authority but limits the ability of the Church to nimbly respond to localized issues. In the nineteenth century, the Oxford Movement promoted an Episcopal succession ecclesiology in which the bishop became the symbol of unity. This ecclesiology persists today in many of The Episcopal Church's ecumenical dialogues, but it risks those very same dialogues by insisting on historical succession. In the early twentieth century, a eucharistic ecclesiology reoriented the Church to the Eucharist celebrated locally under the oversight of the bishop. However, this ecclesiology runs the risk of triumphalism and intermittency that cannot sustain the mission. The ecclesiology most substantially identified with The Episcopal Church today is baptismal ecclesiology. This ecclesiology stresses the ministerial identity of each member of the Church and the common bond of baptism for ecumenical relationships. However, if overstressed, the baptismal identity can result in a "rights" theology that causes greater separation rather than greater communion.

Therefore, a baptismal-eucharistic ecclesiology provides the most robust ecclesiology. The Church gains greater clarity not only by making explicit the inherent connection between baptism and the Eucharist but also their indissoluble bond. The Church also gains wholeness by recognizing our baptismal identity as "Anointed Ones" in Christ as the Crucified-Risen One. Furthermore, the Church recognizes its mission to "make disciples of all nations, baptizing them ... teaching them ... and [remembering] that [Christ] is with [us] always, to the end of the age." Finally, The Episcopal Church articulates a baptismal-eucharistic ecclesiology through its inter-Anglican agreements. Consequently, The Episcopal Church needs to adopt a baptismal-eucharistic ecclesiology explicitly by recognizing the indissoluble bond between baptism, the Eucharist, and the Church.

Diving Deeper

In his introduction to *The Oxford Handbook of Ecclesiology*, the esteemed ecclesiologist Paul Avis defines ecclesiology as the *"comparative, critical, and constructive reflection on the dominant paradigms of the identity of the church."*[71] Ecclesiology is a relatively new branch of theology, having found its disciplinary identity in the early twentieth century. Avis identifies three significant influences on the development of ecclesiology as a theological discipline: the publication of Karl Barth's *Church Dogmatics* in the early twentieth century, the promulgation of *Unitatis Redintegratio* in 1964 during the Second Vatican Council, and the rise of the ecumenical movement.[72]

Of course, ecclesiology begins with Scripture. The New Testament speaks to the nature of the church, which is *ekklesia* in Greek. Of the Gospels, only Matthew explicitly references the Church (Matt 16:18 and 18:17). Many references to the Church exist in the Acts of the Apostles, the epistles, and the Revelation. Paul Minear's classic work *Images of the Church in the New Testament* records ninety-six images of the Church recorded in the New Testament. These images range from minor ones like "salt of the earth" to significant images surrounding the Body of Christ.[73] Like much of biblical theology, these references do not produce a systematic treatment.

---

71. Avis, "Introduction to Ecclesiology," 3.
72. Avis, "Introduction to Ecclesiology," 1-2.
73. Minear, *Images of the Church in the New Testament*, 28-220.

Theologians during the ante-Nicene and Nicene periods, such as Ignatius of Antioch, Tertullian, Cyprian, Ambrose, and Augustine, wrote on the Church with varying degrees of systematicity. The fourth-century creeds spoke of the nature of the Church, producing its primary description as "one, holy, catholic, and apostolic." Medieval theologians, including Peter Lombard and Thomas Aquinas, contributed to a more systematic ecclesiology. However, the birth of modern ecclesiology occurred with the Continental and English reformations and the Roman Catholic Church's Counter-Reformation.[74]

Why is ecclesiology important? First, while the Church acclaims that it is "one," practically, it involves great diversity. This diversity existed long before the Continental and English reformations and even before the Christological controversies of the fourth century. The Church has disagreed, and those disagreements have led to division. Inherent in this diversity is contingency. Avis describes the impact of contingency on the Church.

> Contingency . . . brings with it change—change over time and from place to place—and change generates difference—difference within the one church. Difference creates opposition and conflicts. Oppositions and conflict bring the possibility of error, when we define ourselves over against the other and when we engage in power and struggles within our own church. . . . So contingency brings with it the reality of an ever-increasing diversity and it entails the need for continual reform of abuses and corruption.[75]

Avis does not criticize diversity per se, but he recognizes that it can bring misunderstanding and conflict. Ecclesiology does not seek to

---

74. Avis, "Introduction to Ecclesiology," 5-7.
75. Avis, "Introduction to Ecclesiology," 9.

eliminate diversity but rather to understand how it has impacted the Church throughout history and today. The ecumenical movement's mission has been to encourage dialogue amid this diversity and, thus, work toward healing the divisions within the Church.

Ecclesiology seeks not just to describe the Church but also to reform it. Part of its mission is to call the Church to renewal, which is important for The Episcopal Church. In this chapter, we have discussed different ecclesiologies including their strengths and challenges. This exercise was not merely academic. Without a clear ecclesiology, The Episcopal Church is much more likely to flounder in its attempts at reform. For example, the desire to create a more inclusive experience of communion for those who are not baptized also creates serious ecclesiological questions. The most fundamental question, which this book has sought to answer, is "What is the relationship between baptism, the Eucharist, and the Church?"

To accomplish this call for renewal, ecclesiology must be critical, pastoral, and practical.[76] As Avis underscores, "It will not do for ecclesiology to be merely descriptive or phenomenological—even less, celebratory—of the church. It must always have an ethical cutting edge."[77] A robust ecclesiology is one that can effectively critique the Church.

The baptismal-eucharistic ecclesiology described in this chapter encourages this critical component. Hierarchical ecclesiologies, such as universal, national, and episcopal ecclesiologies, run the risk of minimizing critique in favor of the status quo. The inclusion of all the baptized in the life of the Church, including its governance, ordering, and renewal, provides more opportunities for this critical

---

76. Avis, "Introduction to Ecclesiology," 17–19.
77. Avis, "Introduction to Ecclesiology," 17.

engagement. Directing that critical engagement toward the good of the community in its eucharistic assembly prevents it from being mere self-aggrandizement.

Ecclesiology must also be pastoral. Any ecclesiology that deals only with church structures, organization, and polity lacks the personal quality necessary for the Body of Christ. Christ did not come to save an institution but "to save sinners (1 Tim 1:15)." As the Catechism of The Episcopal Church states, "The mission of the Church is to restore all people to unity with God and each other in Christ."[78] This work of reconciliation is deeply pastoral. It accounts for the real challenges and joys that its members experience.

A baptismal-eucharistic ecclesiology is pastoral. Through the waters of baptism, one is brought into the eucharistic fellowship. As this book has described, baptism's purpose is much more than an exorcistic rite to cleanse one from original sin. As Chrysostom poignantly describes,

> Although many men think that the only gift it [baptism] confers is the remission of sins, we have counted its honors to the number of ten. It is on this account that we baptize even infants, although they are sinless, that they may be given the further gifts of sanctification, justice, filial adoption, and inheritance, that they may be brothers and members of Christ, and become dwelling places for the Spirit.[79]

The gifts of baptism meet the pastoral needs that real people experience, and those gifts are renewed in the eucharistic assembly. Baptism declares one a beloved child of God, and the Eucharist

---

78. 1979BCP, 855.

79. John Chrysostom, "Sermon to the Neophytes" in *Baptism: Ancient Liturgies and Patristic Texts* by André Hamman, 165-171 (New York: Alba House, 1967) 166.

reminds us of that declaration, calls us to repentance, and renews us for mission in the world. Episcopalians have long claimed that even though we may have important differences, we can all come to the eucharistic table together.

Finally, Avis argues that ecclesiology must be practical.[80] Ecclesiology must be more than an academic exercise; it must account for the practices in which the church engages. A robust ecclesiology must engage with what the church does in its everyday mission. It cannot simply be theoretical. These practices can and will involve socially and politically controversial issues as these issues impact members of the church. Therefore, ecclesiology must be prepared to use methods such as ethnography to gather data on these lived practices to better inform the theological analysis undertaken.

A baptismal-eucharistic ecclesiology is deeply connected to the Church's practices. Grounded in the two fundamental sacraments, it takes the practical experiences of Church members seriously. Baptism emphasizes that the lives of all Church members are important, not just the clergy. The Eucharist is the central, communal experience of the Church in which Church members offer their gifts in praise and thanksgiving to God. Of course, the Church has many more practices than just baptism and the Eucharist. Nonetheless, these two central practices are "the summit toward which the activity of the Church is directed [and] the font from which all her power flows."[81]

A critique of a baptismal-eucharistic ecclesiology, like any ecclesiology grounded in the sacramental experience of the Church, is its applicability to non-sacramental ecclesial traditions like Baptists, Charismatics, Pentecostals, and others. This critique is valid. If a

---

80. Avis, "Introduction to Ecclesiology," 17-18.
81. Second Vatican Council, Constitution on the Sacred Liturgy, §10.

tradition believes that baptism is just a public declaration of faith and does not effect a change in a person and their relationship to the church and that the Lord's Supper (i.e., the Eucharist) is only a memorial meal, then a baptismal-eucharistic ecclesiology would inadequately describe that tradition.

However, attempting to find an ecclesiology that fits every Christian tradition would be a significant challenge and likely result in a less-than-robust ecclesiology. "Universal ecclesiologies" have been unsuccessful in adequately describing every ecclesial tradition. Instead, they have often resulted in a swath of Christianity being excluded from the very definition of church. Because Anglicanism generally, and The Episcopal Church more specifically, recognizes the centrality of baptism and the Eucharist as sacraments, a baptismal-eucharistic ecclesiology best describes it, as addressed above. That assertion does not exclude other ecclesial traditions but honors their need for an ecclesiology that best fits their experience.

An additional critique involves the changing nature of The Episcopal Church. The 1979 BCP was promulgated at a time when The Episcopal Church had relatively good access to priests to preside at the Eucharist. While the decline in attendance and membership had already begun, ordinations remained relatively high in most dioceses. However, that trend has significantly changed, especially after the COVID-19 pandemic. The number of parishes without a full-time priest or even a priest able to preside at the Eucharist every Sunday has risen dramatically.

Nonetheless, according to the prayer book, the Eucharist remains "the principal act of Christian worship on the Lord's Day."[82] Bishops have responded to this priest shortage differently. Some are forming bi-vocational priests who can serve parishes while maintaining other

---

82. 1979BCP, 13.

employment. Some are training lay leaders to lead Morning Prayer, returning to the historical model that preceded the 1979 BCP. Others are using Communion from Reserved Sacrament.

Does a baptismal-eucharist ecclesiology adequately describe a church in which the Eucharist cannot be celebrated weekly due to a shortage of priests? That will depend on how the Church responds to this shortage. If the Eucharist continues to be the "principal act of Christian worship on the Lord's Day," in desire if not always in practice, then this ecclesiology remains robust. If Episcopalians continue to understand themselves as essentially a baptized and eucharistic people, even if the celebration of the Eucharist reduces, then this ecclesiology is the most apt one. However, if the Eucharist begins to become a less centralized experience for the average Episcopalian, this ecclesiology will need reconsideration.

A robust ecclesiology is important for an ecclesial tradition's self-understanding and for its relationship with other ecclesial traditions. As discussed above, one of the contributing factors to the growth of ecclesiology as a theological discipline was the growth of the ecumenical movement. As ecclesial traditions began dialoguing, both officially and unofficially, they needed a way to describe the unique contours of their own tradition, i.e., ecclesiology. The next chapter will discuss why a baptismal-eucharistic ecclesiology is the most robust ecclesiology for The Episcopal Church's ecumenical relationships.

CHAPTER FIVE

BAPTISM AND THE EUCHARIST CONNECT THE CHURCH

Ecumenical Perspectives

Thus far, we have considered the indissoluble bond between baptism, the Eucharist, and the Church, as found in Scripture, Church history with a specific focus on The Episcopal Church, the liturgy of The Episcopal Church, and the ecclesiology of The Episcopal Church. This chapter will discuss how baptismal-eucharistic ecclesiology impacts The Episcopal Church's relationship with other ecclesial communities in the wider Church.

Our primary focus will be official ecumenical dialogues and texts as they represent the agreements or attempts at agreement among ecclesial communities in the wider Church. We will begin with the foundational, ecumenical text *Baptism, Eucharist and Ministry* (BEM) produced by the World Council of Churches. We will continue with other contemporary, multilateral and bilateral agreements between The Episcopal Church (or the Anglican Communion as a whole) and other ecclesial communities. Finally, we will examine the discussion within the Wesleyan tradition about Holy Communion as a "converting ordinance" and its impact on conversations about communion without baptism. We will show in this chapter that The Episcopal Church's current ecumenical agreements desire a baptismal-eucharistic ecclesiology as the goal of complete unity in the

Church, and the current proposals for communion without baptism would jeopardize that desired goal.

Laying the Foundation:
Baptism, Eucharist and Ministry

As discussed in chapter two, The Episcopal Church has participated in the ecumenical movement since the movement's inception in 1910 with the Edinburgh World Missionary Conference.[1] After some challenges from two world wars, the World Council of Churches (WCC) emerged as the largest ecumenical organization in Church history. The WCC has met regularly since its inception, producing numerous ecumenical agreements with the goal of complete visible unity.

BEM represents the culmination of this ecumenical work, which has been ongoing for over fifty years, from the first Faith and Order Conference at Lausanne in 1927 to its publication in 1982.[2] While ecumenical discussions have focused on other theological topics, issues surrounding baptism, the Eucharist, and the nature of ministry have been the most challenging issues around which ecclesial communities have desired to find consensus. The Commission that worked on this document included all the confessional traditions of the WCC, the Roman Catholic Church, and other churches that are not yet members.[3]

However, BEM does not represent a consensus among the churches; instead, it is a convergence by which the members of

---

1. For an excellent overview of the history of the Anglican Communion in the ecumenical movement, see Tanner, "Anglican" in *The Oxford Handbook of Ecumenical Studies*, 84-100.
2. BEM, viii.
3. BEM, ix.

the Commission recognize significant levels of agreement. This text reflects that agreement and thus is an essential step toward consensus. The Commission points out that such a consensus, while the goal of ecumenical dialogue, must come from the lived experience of visible unity, which is yet to be realized.[4] The Commission solicited official responses from the churches and compiled those responses. We will first consider the primary text and then The Episcopal Church's responses with some of its closest ecumenical partners.

Baptism, Eucharist and Ministry conveys the critical relationship among its constituent parts by its title. While BEM does not address the issue of communion without baptism directly, as it was not a presenting issue at that time, the order of the reports within the document suggests an inherent order of baptism leading to the Eucharist, which also leads to ministry.[5] We discussed this order as the Ordo in chapter three, and it is represented again in The Episcopal Church's ecumenical conversations.

The Baptism section of BEM not only recognizes baptism as initiation into the Church, the Body of Christ, but also emphasizes baptism as the bond of unity among the churches:

> Through baptism, Christians are brought into union with Christ, with each other and with the Church of every time and place. Our common baptism, which unites us to Christ in faith, is thus a basic bond of unity.... When baptismal unity is realized in one holy, catholic, apostolic Church, a genuine Christian witness can be made to the healing and reconciling love of God. Therefore, our one baptism into

---

4. BEM, ix.

5. A later WCC document, *One Baptism: Toward Mutual Recognition*, does speak directly to communion without baptism. We will consider this document later.

Christ constitutes a call to the churches to overcome their divisions and visibly manifest their fellowship.[6]

This emphasis on baptism as the basis of unity among the churches reflects the baptismal ecclesiology as discussed in chapter four. Baptism not only unites members to Christ but unites them to each other. Unfortunately, Christians do not live into the inherent unity of their baptism due to other divisions within the Church. Nonetheless, the very foundation of the ecumenical movement is that one baptism.

One of the ecumenical movement's most outstanding achievements was the mutual acceptance of baptism among ecclesial traditions. Most Christian traditions recognize each other's baptisms if they were performed using water and the Trinitarian formula.[7] However, not all do. Traditions affirming credobaptism, or believer's baptism, often will not recognize infant baptisms. Also, some traditions do not recognize the baptisms of other churches due to differences in ecclesiology. Nonetheless, this ecumenical agreement signifies a substantial step toward complete unity.

While baptism may be the foundation for the ecumenical movement, complete unity, as expressed in eucharistic communion, is its culmination. BEM expresses this desire for complete unity in the Eucharist:

> The eucharistic communion with Christ who nourishes the life of the Church is at the same time communion within the body of Christ which is the Church. The sharing in one bread and the common cup in a given place demonstrates and effects the oneness of the sharers with Christ and with their

---

6. BEM, 3.
7. For further details, see Heller, *Baptized into Christ*.

fellow sharers in all times and places. *It is in the eucharist that the community of God's people is fully manifested.* Eucharistic celebrations always have to do with the whole Church, and the whole Church is involved in each local eucharistic celebration [italics added].[8]

This ecumenical statement expresses all the churches' deep desire for full eucharistic communion. While the Church's common baptism is the foundation for unity, the Church's divisions are most visible in the lack of full eucharistic communion. The Church's common baptism is not enough. The Church will not know full communion until it experiences it in the Eucharist.

Furthermore, this eucharistic communion recognizes the universal Church and the particular churches within its celebration, as expressed in Afanasiev's eucharistic ecclesiology. The universal Church participates in each local celebration of the Eucharist. Thus, the universal subsists in the particular rather than the particular subsisting in the universal. The Eucharist becomes an eschatological sign of each part of the Church's full communion with each other and all the saints of all times and places.

However, not all ecclesial traditions agree on the nature of the Church.[9] Instead of the Eucharist or even baptism being foundational for their ecclesiologies, some traditions emphasize a confession of Christ as one's personal savior, constituting church membership. Other traditions may recognize baptism and the Eucharist as fundamental building blocks for their ecclesiology but insist on additional criteria such as confessional agreements, doctrinal orthodoxy, or papal or episcopal authority.

---

8. Heller, *Baptized into Christ*, 19.
9. For further details, see Avis, ed., *The Oxford Handbook of Ecclesiology*.

Finally, ecumenical partners have significantly struggled with ministerial structures—particularly the *episkopé*.[10] In the Ministry section, BEM does not address the specific orders of ministry (deacons, priests/presbyters, and bishops) until the third section. The first two sections generously describe the nature of ministry and the interrelation between lay and ordained members of the Church.[11]

When BEM does discuss the *episkopé*, it does so within the context of the Eucharist:

> [The bishop] was ordained and installed to proclaim the Word and preside over the celebration of the eucharist.... Soon, however, the functions were modified. Bishops began increasingly to exercise *episkopé* over several local communities at the same time.... They provide a focus for unity in life and witness within areas comprising several eucharistic communities.[12]

Thus, BEM avoids an "Episcopal Succession" ecclesiology by keeping the work of the *episkopé* firmly rooted in the eucharistic community.[13] While not explicitly stated, this focus on the eucharistic context reflects more than a desire to avoid the contentious issue of apostolic succession, which BEM discusses in section four. Instead, BEM recognizes that the *episkopé* can only be a source of unity among the churches when it remains centered in the eucharistic community.

---

10. The bishop has historically occupied the office of *episkopé*. However, BEM deliberately uses the term *episkopé* rather than bishop to indicate the variety of offices this term envelops. See Commentary (21) in BEM, 25.

11. BEM, 20-24.

12. BEM, 24.

13. See chapter four for details on "Episcopal Succession" ecclesiology.

Otherwise, it becomes an office imposed on the community rather than a ministry born from the community.

Recognizing a common baptism with the goal of full eucharistic communion exercised through the *episkopé*, BEM implies a baptismal-eucharistic ecclesiology. A baptismal ecclesiology fails to account for the goal of full eucharistic communion. A eucharistic ecclesiology deemphasizes common baptism and could encourage clericalism.[14] The *episkopé* is born from baptism and exercises ministry in its eucharistic communion. Thus, an explicit baptismal-eucharistic ecclesiology, joining a baptismal foundation with eucharistic communion as exercised by the *episkopé*, expresses BEM's ecclesiology most robustly.

While BEM represented an unprecedented milestone in ecumenical agreement, it still needed to be accepted by the contributing churches. Therefore, the WCC solicited responses from all members and participating churches and compiled them into a series of volumes. A comprehensive review of this material lies outside of the scope of this work. However, we will consider the responses of The Episcopal Church and its closest ecumenical partners.

By and large, The Episcopal Church received BEM with relatively few significant issues. In 1982, the General Convention charged the Standing Commission on Ecumenical Relations (SCER) to study the text and report back to the General Convention, which they did by soliciting responses from seminaries and dioceses.[15] Regarding the Baptism section, the Commission responded, "The text on Baptism in our survey received the strongest approval, with much agreement that its general approach represents what we understand Baptism

---

14. See chapter four for more details.
15. "Episcopal Church, USA," in *Churches respond to BEM*, 2:57.

to be."[16] However, they expressed concern for the language around rebaptism, baptismal regeneration, and infant baptism.

The Episcopal Church also received the Eucharist section with solid support: "Especially praised were the positions on the centrality of the Eucharist...."[17] They raised concerns about Christ's presence in the elements, the intrinsic relationship between Word and Sacrament, the presidency of the Eucharist, and the sole use of bread and wine as the elements of the Eucharist.[18] Finally, they commended their report for official reception by the 68th General Convention.[19] While some of the issues they raised are important, none directly touch on ecclesiology. Therefore, the Episcopal Church's generally positive reception of BEM also indicates the reception of the implicit baptismal-eucharistic ecclesiology within it.

Other ecumenical partners with The Episcopal Church also expressed a baptismal-eucharistic ecclesiology in their responses to BEM. For example, the Roman Catholic Church stated, "Christian initiation begun in baptism is completed by participation in the eucharist, which is the sacrament that engages and manifests the full reality of the church."[20] Unfortunately, the Roman Catholic Church often lengthens the amount of time in Christian initiation, which is "begun in baptism" and then "completed by participation in the eucharist," by requiring the baptized to reach the "age of reason" as a prerequisite before First Communion.[21] As discussed in chapter two, separating the initiatory rites stretches the indissoluble bond between

---

16. "Episcopal Church, USA," in *Churches respond to BEM*, 2:59.
17. "Episcopal Church, USA," in *Churches respond to BEM*, 2:59.
18. "Episcopal Church, USA," in *Churches respond to BEM*, 2:60.
19. "Episcopal Church, USA," in *Churches respond to BEM*, 2:62.
20. "Roman Catholic Church," in *Churches respond to BEM*, 6:15.
21. The Code of Canon Law, c. 913, §1.

baptism and the Eucharist, with drastic consequences. Nonetheless, this explicit statement of baptismal-eucharistic ecclesiology is laudable from one of The Episcopal Church's closest ecumenical partners.

Another of The Episcopal Church's ecumenical partners, the Orthodox Church, also expresses a baptismal-eucharistic ecclesiology through its desire for stronger language in BEM:

> [BEM] rightly regards baptism 'in the name of the Father and of the Son and of the Holy Spirit' as participation in Christ's death and resurrection; as conversion, pardoning, and cleansing; as gift of the Spirit; as incorporation into the body of Christ and sign of the kingdom. We do wish that the theology expressed in our sacrament of chrismation—that of Pentecostal sealing with God's Spirit—had been affirmed more forthrightly; and that direct entrance into the eucharistic supper of all the fully initiated, infants included, had been upheld as apostolic and normative.[22]

Here, the Orthodox Church excels in expressing a desire for a closer connection between baptism, chrismation, and "direct entrance into the eucharistic supper." The Orthodox Church did not experience the disintegration of Christian initiation in the Western Church because it has preserved the indissoluble bond between baptism, the Eucharist, and the Church. Their desire for stronger language in BEM to convey that bond reflects their desire for a baptismal-eucharistic ecclesiology.

Other ecumenical partners' responses indicate a more implicit rather than explicit desire for a baptismal-eucharistic ecclesiology. For example, the Presbyterian Church (U.S.A.) recognizes baptism

---

22. "Orthodox Church in America," in *Churches respond to BEM*, 3:16.

as a bond of unity among the churches.[23] The Episcopal Church's Lutheran partners agree with the entire text and suggest further work in other areas outside our current discussion.[24] Nonetheless, other ecumenical agreements with these partners express a more explicit baptismal-eucharistic ecclesiology, as discussed below.

However, not all The Episcopal Church's ecumenical partners would fully endorse an explicit baptismal-eucharistic ecclesiology in BEM. For example, the United Church of Christ responded with concerns about baptism alone being considered the sole criterion of membership in the Church. While they affirm baptism as a sign of incorporation into the Church, they also wish to recognize ecclesial communities that do not celebrate the sacraments.[25] In addition, the United Methodist Church recognizes a plurality of views among its members regarding baptism as preparation for full membership in the Church and baptism as preceding the reception of communion.[26] We will consider these ecumenical exceptions more closely in the final section of this chapter.

Even with these exceptions, the responses to BEM indicate a strong preference for a baptismal-eucharistic ecclesiology. The document indicates this ecclesiology implicitly in its ordering and explicitly in its recognition of baptism as our bond of unity and the desire for full communion in the Eucharist. Therefore, BEM lays a strong foundation for a baptismal-eucharistic ecclesiology that connects all ecclesial traditions.

---

23. "Presbyterian Church (U.S.A.)," in *Churches respond to BEM*, 3:191.
24. "Lutheran Church in America," in *Churches respond to BEM*, 1:34.
25. "United Church of Christ [USA]," in *Churches respond to BEM*, 2: 329.
26. "United Methodist Church [USA]," in *Churches respond to BEM*, 2:179-183.

Building on the Foundation: Contemporary Ecumenical Agreements

We will now consider contemporary ecumenical agreements, building on the foundation BEM laid for the Church. We will begin by looking at those ecumenical agreements that have led to full communion with The Episcopal Church. Then, we will consider other ecumenical agreements with partners with whom The Episcopal Church has not yet reached full communion but has shared substantive conversations.

The first ecumenical partners with whom The Episcopal Church agreed to full communion were the Old Catholic Churches in 1931 through the Bonn Agreement.[27] At this point in ecumenical conversations, agreements were straightforward:

1. Each Communion recognizes the catholicity and independence of the other and maintains its own.
2. Each Communion agrees to admit members of the other Communion to participate in the Sacraments.
3. Full Communion does not require from either Communion the acceptance of all doctrinal opinion, sacramental devotion or liturgical practice characteristic of the other, but implies that each believes the other to hold all the essentials of the Christian faith.[28]

Nonetheless, even this simplicity reflects the importance of sacramental sharing. While this agreement does not explicitly reference baptism and the Eucharist, it does imply their presence as the dominical sacraments into which members would be admitted. The Episcopal

---

27. "Full Communion Partners."

28. "Self Select Session on 'Full Communion' Agreements: Mutual Accountability and Difference."

Church made additional full communion agreements with the Philippine Independent Church in 1961 and the Mar Thoma Syrian Church of Malabar, India, in 1979.[29]

However, as time progressed in the ecumenical movement, full communion agreements became more complex. The next full communion agreement with such complexity involved the Evangelical Lutheran Church in America (ELCA). This agreement was codified in the document *Called to Common Mission*, which the General Convention of The Episcopal Church and the Churchwide Assembly of the ELCA approved in 1999. As mentioned above, this document stresses an "Episcopal Succession" ecclesiology. Nonetheless, it does so by laying a firm baptismal foundation.[30] It then builds on that foundation by recognizing full eucharistic sharing as the culmination of the ecumenical process.[31] While episcopal succession may take center stage in this document, it does so only because bishops unite the Church in the Eucharist. Nonetheless, a more explicit baptismal-eucharistic ecclesiology would be preferable in future full communion agreements.

The following full communion agreement with The Episcopal Church was with the Moravian Church in 2006. *Finding Our Delight in the Lord* is the official text describing this agreement. This document states that it builds on earlier ecumenical agreements.[32] Those earlier agreements indicate a baptismal-eucharistic ecclesiology as the basis for full communion: "As the next steps toward that goal [of full communion] we agree: ... on the basis of our common baptism to welcome one another's baptized members to receive sacramental and

---

29. "Full Communion Partners."
30. *Called to Common Mission*, 4-5.
31. *Called to Common Mission*, 6.
32. "Finding Our Delight in the Lord," 4.

other pastoral ministrations . . . ."[33] Once again, baptism provides the foundation for unity, and eucharistic sharing completes it. The Episcopal Church's full communion agreements with the ELCA and the Moravian Church rest on a baptismal-eucharistic ecclesiology.

The Episcopal Church continues to pursue full communion with other ecumenical partners. For example, Anglicans have been discussing full communion with the Orthodox Church since the Lambeth Conference 1920.[34] These discussions also center on a baptismal-eucharistic ecclesiology. For example, *The Moscow Agreed Statement* of 1977 stresses the Eucharist as the source of communion within the Church.[35] In the Dublin Statement of 1987, the Orthodox Church and the Anglican Communion agreed on a "general understanding of baptism" and that "The Eucharist actualizes the Church."[36] Finally, in 2007, the publication of *The Church of the Triune God* marked the most recent Anglican-Orthodox agreement. This publication explicitly states a baptismal-eucharistic ecclesiology:

> In order to come to the table of the Lord for the eucharistic banquet of his Body and Blood we must first be baptised in the name of the Father, the Son and the Holy Spirit (Matthew 28,18-20), and so be conformed to his death and resurrection. . . . Informed by the life and work of God in the baptismal and eucharistic liturgy, the Church always seeks to die and be raised again.[37]

---

33. *Anglican-Moravian Conversations*, 31.

34. Ware and Davey, eds., *Anglican-Orthodox Dialogue: The Moscow Agreed Statement*, 4.

35. Ware and Davey, eds., *Anglican-Orthodox Dialogue: The Moscow Agreed Statement*, 89.

36. *Anglican-Orthodox Dialogue: The Dublin Agreed Statement 1984*, 47.

37. *The Church of the Triune God*, 14-15.

This agreement gives no room for communion without baptism, stating that only baptized persons may come to the eucharistic table. Furthermore, the Church itself rests on both the baptismal and eucharistic liturgies.

Another long-standing ecumenical relationship exists between Anglicans and Roman Catholics. Officially sponsored meetings have occurred in the United States since 1965 and internationally since 1970.[38] While these meetings address many issues, they articulate a baptismal-eucharistic ecclesiology. For example, the 1967 ARC IV Statement on the Eucharist explicitly states, "Baptism is the entrance into the Eucharistic community. In the Holy Eucharist, Christians are united with Christ as the fulfillment and perfection of their baptismal union with Him."[39] *The Final Report*, published in 1982, builds on these preliminary agreements. In particular, the Ministry and Ordination section of the report elucidates a baptismal-eucharistic ecclesiology:

> Christian ministers are members of this redeemed community. Not only do they share through baptism in the priesthood of the people of God, but they are—particularly in presiding at the eucharist—representative of the whole Church in the fulfillment of its priestly vocation of self-offering to God as a living sacrifice (Rom. 12.1).[40]

Baptism provides the entryway into the universal priesthood of Christ. When ordained ministers preside at the Eucharist, they

---

38. *The Final Report of the Anglican—Roman Catholic International Commission*, iv.

39. Bishops' Committee on Ecumenical and Interreligious Affairs. *Documents on Anglican/Roman Catholic Relations*, 3.

40. *The Final Report*, 36.

do so primarily as representatives of the Church in their priestly vocation. This statement articulates a significant reversal from the medieval view of the priest as the sole arbiter of the sacraments. As discussed in chapter two, the indissoluble bond between baptism and the Eucharist profoundly affects one's understanding of ordination and the Church.

The Episcopal Church's dialogues with the Reformed churches exhibit an explicit baptismal-eucharistic ecclesiology. In 1978, the Anglican Consultative Council and the World Alliance of Reformed Churches appointed the Anglican-Reformed Commission to clarify their ecumenical agreement. Due to their meetings, the Commission published *God's Reign and Our Unity* in 1984. In the Baptism section, the Commission explicitly states: "Baptism, by which Christ incorporates us into his life, death and resurrection, is thus, in the strictest sense, constitutive of the Church."[41] Then, in the Eucharist section, the Commission expresses the indissoluble bond between baptism, the Eucharist, and the Church: "Along with baptism, the Eucharist is fundamental to and constitutive of the life of the Church."[42] This agreement does not simply see baptism as the bond of unity for the Church and the Eucharist as the culmination of that unity. It goes further. It recognizes baptism and the Eucharist as "constitutive of the life of the Church." In other words, baptism and the Eucharist make the Church.

In 2006, the General Assembly of the Presbyterian Church (U.S.A.) requested that all its congregations renew their commitments to Word and Sacrament through more profound reflection on the meaning of living a baptismal life.[43] The Sacramental Study Group

---

41. *God's Reign and Our Unity*, 33.
42. *God's Reign and Our Unity*, 44.
43. "Invitation to Christ," Introduction.

wrote a report for their national church indicating the desire for a deepening of the sacramental life of Presbyterians. They concluded their report with a strong statement in favor of a baptismal-eucharistic ecclesiology:

> In conclusion, in our review of the literature the biblical-theological rationales used by those in favor of and opposed to open table practice seem to suggest that the fullest range of meanings of baptism and the Lord's Supper—both God's expansive love and forgiveness and the call to be a community of disciples, the body of Christ in the world—is preserved and embodied through the normative practice of baptism before Eucharist. However, there is a strong biblical crosscurrent, notably in Jesus' inclusive meal practice and his breaking of certain purity laws, that would seem to allow or even call for the disruption of those regular practices if and when those sacramental practices wrongly serve exclusionary purposes.[44]

This conclusion is particularly laudable in that it simultaneously draws on the fullest imagery of baptism and the Eucharist and cautions the Church not to allow them to become exclusionary practices. As discussed in chapter one, the central theme of the Scriptural witness of Jesus' inclusionary meal practices was to reform the eucharistic practices of the congregations to whom they were written. Therefore, the Presbyterian Church is correct in its desire not to see these practices become exclusionary. However, the Church should respond to such exclusionary practices with greater catechesis on the inclusive themes within baptism and the Eucharist rather than resorting to any disruption of the Ordo.

---

44. "Invitation to Christ," 24.

Two recent documents summarize much of the contemporary ecumenical work of the past few years. The first document is *The Vision before Us*, published in 2009 by the Inter-Anglican Standing Commission on Ecumenical Relations (IASCER). The Anglican Consultative Council in 1996 and the Lambeth Conference in 1998 requested that IASCER work toward consistency and coherence concerning the proliferation of bilateral and multilateral agreements in the Anglican Communion.[45] Therefore, this publication seeks to clarify ecumenical conversations and elucidate the consequences of issues on which the Churches of the Anglican Communion might make controversial decisions.

One such issue is communion without baptism. Part two, section four of *The Vision before Us* speaks directly to this issue.[46] The contributors devote considerable space to this issue because they believe it represents "an example of how variations of internal Anglican practice may raise significant questions from ecumenical partners about the integrity of the whole Communion—questions which are not anticipated by those who adopt these practices."[47]

Canon John St-Helier Gibaut, the Moderator of the Faith and Order Section of the WCC, provides an excellent essay describing the many consequences that communion without baptism could have on the Anglican Communion's ecumenical relationships. His conclusion is noteworthy: "Yet this Anglican latitude [toward intercommunion] is embedded in the ecumenical recognition of the deep nexus between baptism and the eucharist, over which even the varying degrees of Christian division cannot prevail. The practice of admitting non-baptised people to the eucharist overthrows a century

---

45. Jones, ed. *The Vision Before Us*, 18.
46. Jones, ed. *The Vision Before Us*, 50-66.
47. Jones, ed. *The Vision Before Us*, 50.

of ecumenical insight and growth."[48] In this excellent conclusion, Canon Gibaut affirms a robust baptismal-eucharistic ecclesiology as the "deep nexus ... which even the varying degrees of Christian division cannot prevail." While he believes a baptismal-eucharistic ecclesiology can prevail against the Church's divisions, he also warns the proponents of communion without baptism about the serious ecumenical repercussions their practice will have should they persist.

Finally, the WCC released a study document entitled *One Baptism: Towards Mutual Recognition* (2011). Unlike BEM, *One Baptism* is a study document rather than a convergence text.[49] Therefore, the WCC gives it to the churches as an opportunity for study and reflection rather than stating it represents a common understanding by all members involved. Nonetheless, this document is ten years in the making and involves the hard work of many scholars working collaboratively. Therefore, this text deserves further study. Much of this text echoes the material already discussed above. Nonetheless, its conclusion aptly summarizes the desire for a baptismal-eucharistic theology to connect the churches:

> Baptism looks beyond itself. As the basis of our common identity in the one body of Christ, it yearns to be completed through the fully eucharistic fellowship of all the members of Christ's body. We should be one at the one table of our one Lord.... The churches are thus called to renewed efforts toward full ecclesial communion, in order that the unity which is theirs in Christ through the waters of baptism may find its fulfillment at his one table.[50]

---

48. Jones, ed. *The Vision Before Us*, 66.
49. *One Baptism: Towards Mutual Recognition*, 1.
50. *One Baptism: Towards Mutual Recognition*, 21.

Baptism yearns for the Eucharist. In like manner, the Church's baptismal unity yearns for completion in eucharistic unity. The ecumenical movement has made great strides in laying a foundation of baptismal unity and building toward full eucharistic communion. The indissoluble bond between baptism and the Eucharist will again unite the Church.

Rearranging the Foundation: Communion as a "Converting Ordinance"?

The Episcopal Church is not the only ecclesial community within which the conversation about communion without baptism has occurred. The Wesleyan tradition has a history of considering communion as a "converting ordinance." This tradition justifies some proponents of communion without baptism, both Wesleyan and Episcopalian, for their position. This section will briefly outline the main conversation around this teaching and its relationship to communion without baptism. Unfortunately, the scope of this work limits a complete treatment of the many issues involved.

In the response from the United Methodist Church in the United States to BEM, they articulated this ongoing conversation within their community:

> United Methodists are not of one mind concerning access to the Lord's table. Who should be invited? Only those baptized? Only the baptized and confirmed? Or any who sincerely desire to come? John Wesley spoke of the eucharist as a 'converting ordinance'. Some find that to be a warrant for inviting all who seek the faith in Christ but have not found it. On the contrary, Wesley, as an Anglican priest, tried to be obedient to the canons, even in a century of sacramental carelessness. He probably

assumed that all people in Great Britain were baptized, and could thus come to holy communion to find conversion.[51]

This response to BEM summarizes the conversation around communion without baptism in the United Methodist Church quite well. It also articulates the similarities between proponents of communion without baptism in both The Episcopal Church and the United Methodist Church in its concern regarding access to the eucharistic table. However, the historical context around Wesley's teaching adds an essential layer to this conversation.

When John Wesley was in ministry in the eighteenth century, the evangelical movement was booming within Britain and the United States.[52] Great evangelical preachers called for conversion, including John Wesley and George Whitefield (both Anglicans) and Jonathan Edwards (a Congregationalist). John Wesley's own conversion story provides an informative illustration. Before his conversion, Wesley was baptized and ordained as a priest. In 1735, he and his brother Charles (the famous hymn writer) traveled to the new colony of Georgia with a group of Moravians. Along the way, the Moravian leader August Spangenberg asked John Wesley if he knew Jesus Christ as his personal savior. This question haunted Wesley during his time in Georgia and his return to Britain. Finally, in 1738, in a chapel on Aldersgate Street in London, he experienced his conversion and could fervently respond that he knew Jesus Christ as his personal savior.

Then, in 1740, Wesley disagreed with his Moravian comrades regarding the ordinances (or sacraments). The Moravians taught that those who had not converted should not be allowed to partake in Holy Communion. For them, not only did a person need to be baptized

---

51. "United Methodist Church [USA]," in *Churches respond to BEM*, 2:183.

52. The following comes from Mullin, *A Short World History of Christianity*, 167-171.

and confirmed, but they also had to have had a conversion experience before receiving communion. Wesley took a broader approach:

> But in later times many have affirmed that the Lord's Supper is not a *converting*, but a *confirming* ordinance.... But experience shows the gross falsehood of that assertion that the Lord's Supper is not a *converting* ordinance. Ye are the witnesses. For many now present know, the very beginning of your *conversion* to God (Perhaps, in some, the first deep *conviction*) was wrought at the Lord's Supper.[53]

Thus, Wesley describes the Lord's Supper as a "converting ordinance." Rather than confirming the conversion experience that one has already had, the Lord's Supper can lead one to that conversion experience. Therefore, he sought to loosen the restriction on the Lord's Supper to allow those who had not yet received a conversion experience to partake.

This historical information is vital as it provides the context in which Wesley described the Lord's Supper as a "converting ordinance." Karen Westerfield-Tucker, Professor of Worship at Boston University, a United Methodist-affiliated school, points out that this controversy between Wesley and the Moravians is the only instance in which Wesley referred to the Lord's Supper as a "converting ordinance."[54] She and the responders to BEM also point out that Wesley taught in a society where infant baptism was the standard practice. Therefore, he was not speaking about communion without baptism.[55]

---

53. Ward and Heitzenrater, eds. *The Works of John Wesley*, 19:158.

54. Westerfield Tucker, "Baptism and Ecumenism: Agreements and Problems on the Journey toward Mutual Recognition," 3.

55. Westerfield Tucker, "Baptism and Ecumenism: Agreements and Problems on the Journey toward Mutual Recognition," and "United Methodist Church [USA]," in *Churches respond to BEM*, 2: 183.

Even Mark Stamm, a proponent of communion without baptism, also recognizes that John Wesley spoke to *"baptized seekers."*[56] However, Stamm argues that unless one can prove that universal baptism was the historical reality, one must give a place to what he calls a "Methodist exception to the baptismal norm."[57] The historicity Stamm requires to consider Wesley's comments to be targeted primarily to a baptized audience is unreasonably rigorous. No historical scenario can withstand that degree of scrutiny. Furthermore, such historical precision would render the entire tradition of the Church null and void. Therefore, Westerfield-Tucker correctly concludes that Wesley's comments are not an argument in favor of communion without baptism.[58]

In fairness to Stamm and others within the Wesleyan tradition, they do not propose a long delay between communion as a "converting ordinance" and baptism.[59] The United Methodist document "By Water and the Spirit: A United Methodist Understanding of Baptism" states, "Unbaptized persons who receive communion should be counseled and nurtured toward baptism *as soon as possible.*"[60] Stamm also goes further to recognize that it would be unlikely for a person to have a conversion experience at their first Eucharist. He believes that, like the solid religious background that preceded the conversion experiences of St. Paul and John Wesley, a similar regularity with the Eucharist would precede a contemporary conversion experience.[61] Stamm also clearly expresses his views as an example of a Methodist

---

56. Stamm, *Let Every Soul be Jesus' Guest*, 64.

57. Stamm, *Let Every Soul be Jesus' Guest*, 64.

58. Westerfield-Tucker, "Baptism and Ecumenism: Agreements and Problems on the Journey toward Mutual Recognition," 4.

59. See Stamm, *Let Every Soul be Jesus' Guest*, 39.

60. "By Water and the Spirit: A United Methodist Understanding of Baptism," 13, italics added.

61. Stamm, *Let Every Soul be Jesus' Guest*, 143.

"exception" to the Ordo of baptism leading to the Eucharist for evangelism.[62]

However, instead of an exception to the Ordo, a fuller view of baptism might be in order, leading to communion. Suppose priests and pastors consistently emphasize the indissoluble bond between baptism and the Eucharist in each service. In that case, they can assure that regular attendees will know that the waters of baptism are open to them at any time. However, if they only emphasize the Eucharist with no apparent connection to baptism, they risk a regular attendee becoming confused. Again, the indissoluble bond between baptism and the Eucharist must become a dynamic and consistent part of the life of the Church.

As The Episcopal Church considers the ecclesiological implications of communion without baptism, it must also remember the implications for its ecumenical relationships. From the beginning of the ecumenical movement, The Episcopal Church has ardently supported full communion in the Church. It has participated in numerous multilateral and bilateral dialogues with its ecumenical partners, leading to significant strides toward full communion. The IASCER rightly cautions proponents of communion without baptism to carefully consider the ecumenical consequences of their position. The indissoluble bond between baptism and the Eucharist is how the Church can ultimately enjoy full communion.

Diving Deeper

This chapter presumes that The Episcopal Church values ecumenism and ecumenical theology. This presumption is based on the long history that The Episcopal Church and other members of the

---

62. Stamm, *Let Every Soul be Jesus' Guest*, 19.

Anglican Communion have had with the ecumenical movement. From the first Lambeth Conference in 1867, reunion with other churches was a matter of serious discussion. In 1886, bishops of The Episcopal Church adopted the Chicago Quadrilateral, and two years later, the Lambeth Conference adopted these four principles for ecumenical reunion.[63] These efforts predate the Edinburgh Missionary Conference of 1910, which is often cited as the start of the ecumenical movement.

In 1920, Anglican bishops across the Communion gathered in Lambeth after the devasting First World War. The first eight resolutions addressed those horrors. In response, the bishops called for the full, visible unity of the Christian Church. They produced one of the longest resolutions from any Lambeth Conference, "Resolution 9— Reunion of Christendom."[64] Based on a common baptism, they called for the "visible unity of the whole Church." While they believed the episcopacy to be "the best instrument for maintaining the unity and continuity of the Church," they did not ask that "any one Communion should consent to be absorbed into another. We do ask that all should unite in a new and great endeavour to recover and to manifest to the world the unity of the Body of Christ for which he prayed."[65]

From this endeavor, the Anglican Communion and The Episcopal Church have indicated their ongoing and exuberant support for ecumenism, as evidenced by the numerous multilateral and bilateral dialogues mentioned above. This support continues today. As recently as April 30, 2024, United Methodist General Conference members

---

63. Tanner, "Anglican," 85; see also, 1979BCP, 877-878.

64. Tanner, "Anglican," 87.

65. "Resolution 9 – Reunion of Christendom," Anglican Communion, accessed May 6, 2024, https://www.anglicancommunion.org/resources/document-library/lambeth-conference/1920/resolution-9-reunion-of-christendom?author=Lambeth+Conference.

approved full communion with The Episcopal Church.[66] The 2024 General Convention reaffirmed the goal of full communion with the United Methodist Church.[67]

Much work has been done since the ecumenical movement's inception. Is it worth it? While numerous bilateral and multilateral dialogues and even some full communion agreements have occurred, is the Church substantially closer to full, visible unity today than it was at the turn of the last century? Concerns continue about the goals of the ecumenical movement. On the one hand, some might wonder, "Will full, visible unity lead to relativizing important doctrines and practices to such an extent that individual traditions lose their distinctiveness?" Others may feel that it is enough that Christians agree to work together on missional projects and have achieved enough appreciation for each other's differences that further attempts at unity are unnecessary. "Are all these theological conversations helpful? Can't we agree to disagree?"

Unsurprisingly, the renowned Anglican ecumenist Paul Avis believes that such theological dialogues and the discipline of ecumenical theology are essential for the Church. He offers five methodological qualities that mark substantive theological engagement among ecclesial traditions. First, the dialogue should be "scholarly and rigorous and digs deep, infused with empathy, into the bedrock of the traditions." It is not enough for dialogue to be concerned only with superficial issues. It requires theological rigor. It also "avoids deliberately vague

---

66. "Full Communion with Episcopalians gets closer," UM News, accessed May 6, 2024, https://www.umnews.org/en/news/full-communion-with-episcopalians-gets-closer.

67. "A049 Affirming the Goal of Full Communion between The Episcopal Church and the United Methodist Church," The General Convention of The Episcopal Church, accessed July 26, 2024, https://www.vbinder.net/resolutions/495?house=HD&lang=en.

or ambiguous formulations that can later be subjected to diverse interpretations and even haggled over." Sometimes, the desire to find consensus eliminates precision, confusing the reception of the dialogues. The dialogues must also be "truly representative of the spectrum of the traditions within the churches concerned, rather than a gathering of rather like-minded and amenable, but not fully representative, individuals." Disagreement on important matters occurs within ecclesial traditions. Therefore, a spectrum of perspectives on issues should be represented. Dialogue "follows a cumulative method and trajectory that consolidates and builds on the progress that has already been made, before attempting to break fresh ground." This quality is especially critical as the timespan for ecumenical dialogues has grown to involve multiple generations. Finally, ecumenical dialogue "tests its emerging conclusions, and at the same time facilitates the process of formal reception that will eventually be needed, by consulting with the constituencies that it represents *in via* rather than, as often happens, presenting a *fait accompli* to the sponsoring churches, which leaves little room for second thought."[68]

While Avis suggests these methodological qualities for ecumenical dialogue, they are equally helpful for intra-ecclesial dialogue, such as the present issue of communion without baptism. Unfortunately, these approaches have not taken place. Praxis has preceded dialogue as many Episcopal churches engage in communion without baptism, while substantive theological discussion remains minimal.

One of the contributing factors to this lack of substantive theological engagement is a lack of organizational structure in which it could occur. The ecumenical movement has resulted in many commissions that engage in dialogue. The Anglican Communion has developed its "instruments of unity," which are

---

68. Avis, *Reconciling Theology*, 7.

formal structures in which dialogue can occur. However, similar structures in The Episcopal Church are not conducive to dialogue or lack representation.

Historically, the General Convention of The Episcopal Church has been the place where legislation to repeal the canon prohibiting communion to the unbaptized has been attempted. However, while the General Convention offers a balanced and representative synod for legislative matters, it cannot afford the time for substantive dialogue. Speakers are given mere minutes to make their case for or against issues due to the press for time. Furthermore, the legislative ethos forces dialogue into a binary, for or against, approach. These qualities impede productive dialogue.

Another avenue for substantive dialogue within The Episcopal Church is the House of Bishops Theology Committee. This committee often includes rigorous and scholarly discussion, but it lacks representation. While members of other orders of ministry sit on the committee, it remains a committee of one order of ministry. Nonetheless, it could act as a model for other such endeavors.

The Standing Commission on Liturgy and Music is another avenue for dialogue. Its membership is composed of all orders of ministry and is, thus, more representative. However, its membership is limited and appointed. Furthermore, its agenda is often overloaded as its work must occur in the triennium between General Conventions. Therefore, sustained dialogue becomes a challenge. The Episcopal Church needs to create better structures for internal dialogue on critical issues that are representative and permit sustained engagement.

In his book *Reshaping Ecumenical Theology*, Avis offers four criteria for robust ecumenical theology. While concerned with ecumenical dialogue, these criteria are essential for any theological dialogue, including the issue of communion without baptism. First,

Avis says, "Ecumenical theology must be *coherent*."[69] The arguments must follow each other. The discussion in this book has endeavored to be coherent in showing that the traditional Ordo of a unitive rite of initiation most fully achieves the ecclesiology of The Episcopal Church within those rites. Attempts to separate those rites and rearrange them, both historically and in the issue of communion without baptism, lose coherency and result in theological gaps and confusion.

Secondly, Avis posits, "Ecumenical theology should be *credible*."[70] In other words, it must be realistic and consider the tradition's existing values, beliefs, and structures. This book has gone to great lengths to establish credibility. Through its analysis of Scripture, church history, liturgical theology, and ecclesiology, it has made the case that the traditional Ordo offers the most fulsome ecclesiology. Proponents of communion without baptism have yet to formally articulate how their proposal would impact the ecclesiology of The Episcopal Church. Essential questions on membership in the Body of Christ have been left unarticulated, presumably under the presumption that baptism would occur quickly.[71] Nonetheless, these issues and others need to be addressed.

Lest anyone believe that ecumenical theology intends only to preserve the status quo, Avis also declares, "Ecumenical theology must be *critical*. That is to say, it should be rigorously self-reflective so that it is critical not only of the material, the ideas or the arguments that it is working on, but also of its own presuppositions."[72] Proponents of

---

69. Avis, *Reshaping Ecumenical Theology*, 42 (italics in original).

70. Avis, *Reshaping Ecumenical Theology*, 42 (italics in original).

71. Mark Stamm, a Methodist pastor, has made this argument. See Stamm, *Let Every Soul be Jesus' Guest*, 39. However, Episcopal proponents have not spoken to the time between communion and baptism.

72. Avis, *Reshaping Ecumenical Theology*, 42 (italics in original).

communion without baptism have raised significant critiques. As mentioned throughout this book, their critiques of baptism as a purity rite and of exclusionary practices such as fencing the table are not only correct but essential for the Church to accept. While the use of the traditional Ordo need not employ these practices, its proponents must remain attentive to these crucial critiques.

Finally, Avis states that "Ecumenical theology should be *constructive*."[73] Productive dialogue does more than point out the deficiencies. It also contributes positively to the ongoing work. This book seeks to take the valid critiques that proponents of communion without baptism have made and find creative and pastoral ways to address them while maintaining the traditional Ordo. The reality that this issue exists in the Church points to the need for creative catechesis on its central rites of baptism and the Eucharist.

The methodologies and principles of ecumenical theology offer tools for effective theological dialogues. The issue of communion without baptism deserves the most robust dialogue possible, as its implications for the ecclesiology of The Episcopal Church are considerable. Too little substantive dialogue has occurred to make such a crucial change. The rush to legislative action should be avoided, and structures should be developed to engage more conversation on this issue.

The Episcopal Church has been at the forefront of the ecumenical movement. The desire to obey Christ's command that "they may all be one (John 17:21a)" has been central to its life. Many dedicated Episcopalians have given much energy to progressing the goals of the ecumenical movement. As discussed above, numerous bilateral and multilateral agreements have been forged based on baptismal-eucharistic ecclesiology. The official endorsement of communion

---

73. Avis, *Reshaping Ecumenical Theology*, 43 (italics in original).

without baptism could seriously jeopardize those agreements and the relationships on which they have been built. Due consideration must be given to the impact on those relationships as part of any decision-making process.

CONCLUSION

Throughout this work, we have looked at one of the most critical issues facing The Episcopal Church today: the relationship between baptism, the Eucharist, and the Church. We have considered this issue from the perspective of Scripture, the history of the Church generally and then specifically in The Episcopal Church, the baptismal-eucharistic liturgical theology of the BCP, the baptismal-eucharistic ecclesiology of The Episcopal Church, and its impact on the ecumenical movement. From each perspective, we have argued that the indissoluble bond between baptism and the Eucharist makes the Church.

The center of this argument rests on God's redeeming love through Christ for all humanity. The Church's primary mission is to proclaim that Good News to the world. At times, ecclesial traditions within the Church have failed in this mission, even in their good intentions. An example is the historical practice of "fencing" in which the communion rail was guarded not only from the unbaptized but from any deemed "unworthy" by the members of that community. Such practices are against the inclusive practices of Jesus' table fellowship, his overall ministry, and his death and resurrection. Christ came to bring everyone—male and female, rich and poor, black and white, gay and straight, sinner and saint—into the reign of God. The Church's mission is to proclaim that Good News to everyone through Word and Sacrament. Any practice that attempts to exclude someone from that Good News deserves condemnation. We have argued that baptism is a sacrament of inclusion through which one not only joins the Church but becomes a part of the Body of Christ and enters the very life of the Triune God.

In addition, we have argued in favor of the traditional Ordo that reunites baptism and communion as a single event. However, opportunities arise in communities when exceptions must occur. These pastoral exceptions permit a gracious response. For example, a priest or pastor cannot know the baptismal status of every person who comes to receive communion, and that is not the time to inquire. Turning someone away from the communion table, regardless of that person's baptismal status, fails to model Christ's inclusive practice. God's grace is sufficient if God has drawn that person to the communion table. The minister's role is not to protect the table but to serve at it.

However, these pastoral responses are different from public policies. Such public policies include changing The Episcopal Church's canons. They also include public invitations to communion, either written or verbal, that do not mention baptism. These invitations are not a pastoral response to an individual need. They are a public declaration of a theological position. Invitations to communion can uphold the traditional Ordo and be pastoral. Terse invitations should be avoided: "<u>Only</u> baptized persons may receive communion in this church." Such an invitation walks very closely to abhorrent exclusionary practices. Instead, an invitation that honors the bond between baptism and the Eucharist while also offering an invitation for a blessing to those not ready for that bond with Christ and his Church would be more appropriate: "We journey from the baptismal waters our Lord sanctified with his baptism to the table our Lord has prepared for those who love him. All who have joined our Lord in baptism are welcome to join him at this table. We would love to talk with you if you have questions or would like more information about baptism. Please also join us at this table for a blessing." With creativity and an underlying passion for the deep connections between baptism and the Eucharist, we can ensure that everyone feels welcome in our services.

Another important pastoral concern involves the people being invited to receive communion without baptism. Do they know the commitment they are making when they receive communion? The baptismal rite is clear that one becomes identified with Christ, the Crucified-Risen One, through its waters and also a member of the Church, the Body of Christ. The eucharistic rite presumes this fact. Thus, the postcommunion prayers say, "Eternal God, heavenly Father, you have graciously accepted us as living members of your Son our Saviour Jesus Christ"[1] or "Almighty and everliving God, we thank you ... for assuring us in these holy mysteries that we are living members of the Body of your Son, and heirs of your eternal kingdom."[2] As already discussed, these prayers have strong ecclesiological implications for those receiving communion.

What is the status in the Body of Christ of those who receive communion without baptism? Are they members or not? The postcommunion prayers would suggest that they are. Do they know they have made that commitment by receiving communion? This is not an argument that one must have full, cognitive capacity before receiving communion. Obviously, infants do not, and this essay has argued in favor of infant communion. However, in the case of infants and young children, the parents and godparents make that commitment on their behalf. For older children and adults, is it a pastoral response to offer a public invitation to them to receive communion without fully informing them of the commitment they are about to make by doing so?

---

1. 1979BCP, 365.
2. 1979BCP, 366.

These pastoral concerns are as important as the theological concerns. The traditional Ordo ensures that baptismal candidates or their parents are clear about the commitment they are making to Christ and Christ's Body, the Church, before receiving communion. Then, they immediately enter the eucharistic assembly as full members of the Body of Christ and are joined with Christ anew through communion.

The indissoluble bond between baptism and the Eucharist makes the Church. This bond is a deep bond that not only connects baptism and the Eucharist but also connects each member of the Church to them. Through this bond, each member is connected to particular churches and the universal Church. Through this bond, Christ connects each member with himself by his death and resurrection. Through this bond, he also connects each member with all of the life God has created. Finally, through this bond, he connects each member with the very inner life of the Triune God.

Therefore, the Church dares not risk breaking this bond. The historical consequences of the Church's attempt to do so are evident—a diminishment of baptism, exaggerated eucharistic realism, and a rise in clericalism. The bond between baptism and the Eucharist empowers the Church in its mission and ministry. All members of the Church, lay and ordained, recognize the full potential of their ministries through this bond. Therefore, proposals to break this bond through an attempt to reverse it would have severe implications for the ecclesiology of The Episcopal Church.

The Triune God invites all humanity into full communion through Christ in the power of the Holy Spirit. Baptism leads us into a new identity in Christ, and chrismation anoints us with the Holy Spirit as a priestly people to participate fully in the eucharistic assembly, the Church, as the Body of Christ. An explicit baptismal-eucharistic ecclesiology provides the most robust expression for this indissoluble bond. May The Episcopal Church continue affirming that baptism, the Eucharist, and the Church are bound together.

BIBLIOGRAPHY

"A049 Affirming the Goal of Full Communion between The Episcopal Church and the United Methodist Church," The General Convention of The Episcopal Church, accessed May 6, 2024, https://www.vbinder.net/resolutions/495?house=HD&lang=en.

"Acts of General Convention D084," accessed May 2, 2024, at http://www.episcopalarchives.org/cgi-bin/acts/acts_resolution.pl?resolution=2006-D084.

Afanasiev, Nicholas. *The Church of the Holy Spirit*. Translated by Vitaly Permiakov. Notre Dame, IN: University of Notre Dame Press, 2007.

_____. "The Church which presides in love." In *The Primacy of Peter*, 57-110. London: The Faith Press, 1963.

Anglican-Moravian Conversations. London: Council for Christian Unity of the General Synod of the Church of England, 1996.

Anglican-Orthodox Dialogue: The Dublin Agreed Statement 1984. Crestwood, NY: St. Vladimir's Seminary, 1985.

Annotated Constitution and Canons, 1991 Supplement. New York: The General Convention, 1991.

Augustine. "Sermon on Easter Morning." In *Message of the Fathers of the Church*, volume 6, edited by Thomas M. Finn, 158-160. Collegeville, MN: The Liturgical Press, 1992.

Avis, Paul. *The Anglican Understanding of the Church*. London: SPCK, 2000.

_____. "Introduction to Ecclesiology." In *The Oxford Handbook of Ecclesiology*, 1-30. Oxford: Oxford University Press, 2018.

_____, ed. *The Oxford Handbook of Ecclesiology*. Oxford: Oxford University Press, 2018.

_____. *Reconciling Theology*. London: SCM Press, 2022.

_____. *Reshaping Ecumenical Theology: The Church Made Whole?* New York: T&T Clark International, 2010.

Baptism, Eucharist and Ministry. Geneva: World Council of Churches, 1982.

Barth, Karl. *The Christian Life, Church Dogmatics IV,4 Lecture Fragments.* Translated by Geoffrey W. Bromiley. Grand Rapids, MI: William B. Eerdmans Publishing Company, 1981.

———. *The Teaching of the Church Regarding Baptism.* Translated by Ernest A. Payne. London: SCM Press, 1948.

Bishops' Committee on Ecumenical and Interreligious Affairs. *Documents on Anglican/Roman Catholic Relations.* Washington, DC: United States Catholic Conference, 1972.

Bobertz, Charles A. "Ritual Eucharist Within Narrative: A Comparison of *Didache* 9-10 with *Mark* 6:31-44; 8:1-9." In *Studia Patristica.* Edited by J. Baun, A. Cameron, M. Edwards and M. Vinzent, 93-99. Leuven, Belgium: Peeters, 2010.

Bogert-Winkler, Hilary. "The Open Debate on Open Communion in The Episcopal Church." *Journal of Anglican Studies* 21 (2023): 235-245.

The Book of Common Prayer and Administration of the Sacraments and Other Rites and Ceremonies of the Church: together with the Psalter or Psalms of David according to the Use of the Episcopal Church. New York: Church Hymnal Corp., 1979.

Bradshaw, Paul F. *Eucharistic Origins.* NY: Oxford University Press, 2004.

———. *Reconstructing Early Christian Worship.* London: Society for Promoting Christian Knowledge, 2009.

———. *The Search for the Origins of Christian Worship: Sources and Methods for the Study of Early Liturgy.* London: SPCK, 1992.

Brown, Raymond E. *An Introduction to the New Testament.* New York: Doubleday, 1997.

"By Water and the Spirit: A United Methodist Understanding of Baptism." Accessed May 2, 2024, at https://www.umc.org/en/content/by-water-and-the-spirit-a-united-methodist-understanding-of-baptism.

Called to Common Mission. Chicago, IL: Evangelical Lutheran Church of America, 1999.

The Canons of the Episcopal Church. Accessed May 2, 2024, at https://generalconvention.org/constitution-and-canons.

"The Chicago Statement on Biblical Inerrancy." Oakland, CA: International Council on Biblical Inerrancy, n.d. Accessed March 11, 2024, at https://library.dts.edu/Pages/TL/Special/ICBI_1.pdf.

Childs, Brevard. *Introduction to the Old Testament as Scripture*. Philadelphia: Fortress Press, 1979.

Chorley, E. Clowes. "The New American Prayer Book: Its History and Contents." Project Canterbury. Accessed May 2, 2024, at http://anglicanhistory.org/bcp/chorley1929/07.html.

Christmas, Henry, ed. *The Works of Nicholas Ridley*. Cambridge: The University Press, 1843.

Chupungco, Anscar J. *Cultural Adaptation of the Liturgy*. New York: Paulist Press, 1982.

———. "Liturgy and Inculturation." In *Fundamental Liturgy*, II:337–75. Handbook for Liturgical Studies. Collegeville, Minnesota: Liturgical Press, 1998.

The Church of the Triune God. London: The Anglican Communion Office, 2006.

Cochrane, Arthur C. *Eating and Drinking with Jesus*. Philadelphia: The Westminster Press, 1974.

The Code of Canon Law. Accessed May 2, 2024, at https://www.vatican.va/archive/cod-iuris-canonici/eng/documents/cic_lib4-cann879-958_en.html#Art._2.

Coleman, Roger, ed. *Resolutions of the Twelve Lambeth Conferences 1867 – 1988*. Toronto: Anglican Book Centre, 1992.

Constitution and Canons. New York: General Convention, 1985.

Constitution and Canons. New York: Church Publishing Incorporated, 2009.

Constitution and Canons. New York: General Convention, 2022.

Cummings, Edward, ed. *The Book of Common Prayer: The Texts of 1549, 1559, and 1662*. Oxford: Oxford University Press, 2011.

Denysenko, Nicholas E. 2021. "Renewing Alexander Schmemann's Liturgical Legacy." *St Vladimir's Theological Quarterly* 65 (1–2): 153–86.

"The Didache." In *Documents of the Baptismal Liturgy*, edited by E. C. Whitaker, revised and expanded by Maxwell E. Johnson, 1–2. Collegeville, MN: Liturgical Press, 2003.

"Didascalia Apostolorum." In *Documents of the Baptismal Liturgy*, edited by E. C. Whitaker, revised and expanded by Maxwell E. Johnson, 14-15. Collegeville, MN: Liturgical Press, 2003.

Dix, Gregory. *The Shape of the Liturgy*. Westminster: Dacre Press, 1945.

———. *The Theology of Confirmation in Relation to Baptism*. Westminster: Dacre Press, 1946.

Edmonson, Stephen. *Liturgical Theology Revisited: Open Table, Baptism, Church*. Eugene, OR: Cascade Books, 2015.

———. "Opening the Table: The Body of Christ and God's Prodigal Grace." *Anglican Theological Review* 91, no. 2 (Spring 2009): 213-234.

"The English Text of *Apostolicae Curae*." In R. William Franklin, ed. *Anglican Orders*, 127-137. Harrisburg, PA: Morehouse Publishing, 1996.

Erickson, John H. "The Church in modern Orthodox thought: towards a baptismal ecclesiology." *International Journal for the Study of the Christian Church* 11 (May-August 2011): 2-3, 137-151.

The Eucharist: Sacrament of Unity. London: Church House Publishing, 2001.

"Eusebius Gallicanus (Seventh Century) or Faustus of Riez (Fifth Century) Homily 29, on Pentecost, 1-2." In *Documents of the Baptismal Liturgy*, edited by E. C. Whitaker, revised and expanded by Maxwell E. Johnson, 257-258. Collegeville, MN: Liturgical Press, 2003.

Fabian, Richard. "First the Table, then the Font." The Association of Anglican Musicians, 2002. Accessed May 2, 2024, at https://www.saintgregorys.org/uploads/2/4/2/6/24265184/firstthetable.pdf.

Fagerburg, David W. *Theologia Prima: What is Liturgical Theology?* Chicago: Hillenbrand Books, 2004.

Ferguson, Everett. *Baptism in the Early Church*. Grand Rapids, MI: William B. Eerdmans Publishing Company, 2008.

The Final Report of the Anglican—Roman Catholic International Commission. Cincinnati, OH: Forward Movement Publications, 1982.

"Finding Our Delight in the Lord." Accessed May 2, 2024, at https://www.episcopalchurch.org/wp-content/uploads/sites/2/2020/07/eir_finding_our_delight_official_text.pdf.

Fisher, J.D.C. *Christian Initiation: Baptism in the Medieval West*. London: SPCK, 1965.

_____. *Christian Initiation: The Reformation Period*. London: SPCK, 1970.

Flusser, David. "Paul's Jewish Christian Opponents in the *Didache*." In *Gilgul*. Edited by S. Shaked, D. Shulman and G.G. Stroumsa, 71-90. Leiden, Netherlands: E. J. Brill, 1987.

"Full Communion with Episcopalians gets closer." UM News. Accessed May 6, 2024, at https://www.umnews.org/en/news/full-communion-with-episcopalians-gets-closer.

"Full Communion Partners." Accessed May 2, 2024, at https://www.episcopalchurch.org/ministries/ecumenical-interreligious/full-communion-partners.

"General Convention/Executive Council," The Episcopal Church. Accessed May 2, 2024, at http://episcopalchurch.org/page/general-convention-executive-council.

Gibson, Paul. "A Baptismal Ecclesiology – Some Questions." In *Equipping the Saints: Ordination in Anglicanism Today*, eds., Ronald L. Dowling and David R. Holeton. Dublin: The Columbia Press, 2006.

God's Reign and Our Unity. London: SPCK, 1984.

Hatchett, Marion. *Commentary on the American Prayer Book*. New York: Harper Collins, 1995.

Heller, Dagmar. *Baptized into Christ: A Guide to the Ecumenical Discussion on Baptism*. Geneva: World Council of Churches Publications, 2012.

Hofius, Otfried. "Herrenmahl und Herrenmahlsparadosis: Erwagungen zu 1 Kor 11, 23b-25." In *Paulusstudien*. Tubingen: Mohr-Siebeck, 1994.

"Invitation to Christ." Accessed May 2, 2024, at https://www.presbyterianmission.org/wp-content/uploads/Invitation-to-Christ.pdf.

Irenaeus. "Against the Heresies." In *Irenaeus of Lyons on Baptism and Eucharist*. Nottingham: Grove Books Limited, 1991.

Irwin, Kevin W. *Context and Text: Method in Liturgical Theology*, revised edition. Collegeville, MN: The Liturgical Press, 2018.

Jefferson, Thomas. *The Life and Morals of Jesus of Nazareth Extracted Textually from the Gospels in Greek, Latin, French, and English*. Washington, DC: Smithsonian, n.d. Accessed March 12, 2024, at https://americanhistory.si.edu/jeffersonbible.

John Chrysostom. "Sermon to the Neophytes." In *Baptism: Ancient Liturgies and Patristic Texts* by André Hamman, 165-171. New York: Alba House, 1967.

"John the Deacon." In *Documents of the Baptismal Liturgy*, edited by E. C. Whitaker, revised and expanded by Maxwell E. Johnson, 208-212. Collegeville, MN: Liturgical Press, 2003.

Johnson, Maxwell E. *The Rites of Christian Initiation*. Revised Ed. Collegeville, MN: Liturgical Press, 2007.

Jones, Sarah Rowland, ed. *The Vision Before Us*. London: The Anglican Communion Office, 2009.

Kavanagh, Aidan. *On Liturgical Theology*. Collegeville, MN: The Liturgical Press, 1992.

Kavanagh, Aidan. "Unfinished and Unbegun Revisited: The Rite of Christian Initiation of Adults." In *Living Water, Sealing Spirit*, edited by Maxwell E. Johnson, 259-273. Collegeville, MN: The Liturgical Press, 1995.

Kaye, Bruce. *An Introduction to World Anglicanism*. Cambridge: Cambridge University Press, 2008.

Kilmartin, Edward J. *The Eucharist in the Primitive Church*. Englewood Cliffs, NJ: Prentice-Hall, 1965.

_____. *The Eucharist in the West*. Collegeville, MN: The Liturgical Press, 1998.

Knight, Douglas, ed. *Methods of Biblical Interpretation*. Nashville, TN: Abingdon Press, 2004.

Krentz, Edgar. *The Historical-Critical Method*. Philadelphia: Fortress Press, 1975.

Larson-Miller, Lizette. "Baptismal Ecclesiology without Baptism?" In *Drenched in Grace: Essays in Baptismal Ecclesiology Inspired by the Work and Ministry of Louis Weil*, eds. Lizette Larson-Miller and Walter Knowles. Eugene, OR: Pickwick Publications, 2013.

_____. *Sacramentality Renewed: Contemporary Conversations in Sacramental Theology*. Collegeville, MN: Liturgical Press, 2016.

Lathrop, Gordon. *The Four Gospels on Sunday*. Minneapolis: Fortress Press, 2012.

_____. *Holy Things: A Liturgical Theology*. Minneapolis: Fortress Press, 1998.

LaVerdiere, Eugene. *The Eucharist in the New Testament and the Early Church*. Collegeville, MN: The Liturgical Press, 1996.

"The Letter of Pope Innocent to Decentius, 416." In *Documents of the Baptismal Liturgy*, edited by E. C. Whitaker, revised and expanded by Maxwell E. Johnson, 205-206. Collegeville, MN: Liturgical Press, 2003.

MacCulloch, Diarmaid. *The Reformation*. New York: Viking Penguin Group, 2004.

Marcus, Joel. "Mark – Interpreter of Paul." *New Testament Studies* 46 (2000): 473-487.

Marshall, Paul V. *Prayer Book Parallels*. Volume One. New York: The Church Hymnal Corporation, 1989.

McGowan, Andrew. "The Meals of Jesus and the Meals of the Church: Eucharistic Origins and Admission to Communion." In *Studia Liturgica Diversa: Essays in Honor of Paul F. Bradshaw*, edited by Maxwell E. Johnson and L. Edward Phillips, 101-115. Portland, OR: Pastoral Press, 2004.

McKnight, Edgar V. *What is Form Criticism?* Philadelphia: Fortress Press, 1969.

McPartlan, Paul. *The Eucharist Makes the Church*. Edinburgh: T&T Clark, 1993.

Meyers, Ruth A. *Continuing the Reformation*. New York: Church Publishing, 1997.

_____. "The Renewal of Christian Initiation in The Episcopal Church, 1928-1979." PhD diss., University of Notre Dame, 1992.

Miles, Sara. *Take This Bread*. New York: Ballantine Books, 2007.

Minear, Paul. *Images of the Church in the New Testament*. Louisville, KY: Westminster John Knox Press, 1960, reprint 2004.

Mitchell, Leonel L. *Praying Shapes Believing*. Harrisburg, PA: Morehouse Publishing, 1985.

Morris, Richard A., Fairweather, Eugene R., Griffiss, J.E. and Mollegen, Albert T. "A Report on The Validity of the Philadelphia Ordinations." In *The Ordination of Women: Pro and Con*, edited by Michael P. Hamilton and Nancy S. Montgomery, 179-195. New York: Morehouse-Barlow Co., 1975.

Mullin, Robert Bruce. *A Short World History of Christianity*. Louisville, KY: Westminster John Knox Press, 2008.

One Baptism: Towards Mutual Recognition. Geneva: World Council of Churches, 2011.

Patterson, M.W. *A History of the Church of England*. 2nd ed. New York: Longmans, Green and Co., 1912.

Peterson, Cheryl. "Font to Table or Table to Font?" *Lutheran Forum* 42, no. 2 (Sum 2008): 46-51.

Prayer Book Studies I: Baptism and Confirmation. New York: The Church Pension Fund, 1950.

Prayer Book Studies 18: On Baptism and Confirmation. New York: The Church Pension Fund, 1970.

Prayer Book Studies 26: Holy Baptism. New York: The Church Hymnal Corporation, 1973.

Prichard, Robert. *A History of the Episcopal Church*. Revised edition. New York: Morehouse Publishing, 1999.

"Resolution 9 – Reunion of Christendom." Anglican Communion. Accessed May 6, 2024, at https://www.anglicancommunion.org/resources/document-library/lambeth-conference/1920/resolution-9-reunion-of-christendom?author=Lambeth+Conference.

Sanders, James. *Canon and Community: A Guide to Canonical Criticism.* Philadelphia: Fortress Press, 1984.

Schmemann, Alexander. *Introduction to Liturgical Theology.* Translated by Asheleigh E. Moorehouse. Crestwood, NY: St. Vladimir's Seminary Press, 2003.

Second Vatican Council, Constitution on the Sacred Liturgy *Sacrosanctum concilium* (4 December 1963). Accessed April 30, 2024, at https://www.vatican.va/archive/hist_councils/ii_vatican_council/documents/vat-ii_const_19631204_sacrosanctum-concilium_en.html.

"Self Select Session on 'Full Communion' Agreements: Mutual Accountability and Difference,'" Lambeth Conference 2008. Accessed May 2, 2024, at http://www.anglicancommunion.org/media/107098/IASCER-Resolutions-arising-from-the-2008-meeting.pdf

Spinks, Bryan D. "Mis-Shapen: Gregory Dix and the Four-Action Shape of the Liturgy." *Lutheran Quarterly* 4, no. 2 (1990): 161–77.

Stamm, Mark. *Let Every Soul be Jesus' Guest.* Nashville, TN: Abingdon Press, 2006.

Steiner, Bruce E. *Samuel Seabury.* Oberlin, OH: Oberlin Printing Company, 1971.

Strout, Shawn. "Jesus' Table Fellowship, Baptism, and the Eucharist." *The Anglican Theological Review* 98, no. 3 (Sum 2016): 479-934.

———. "*Of Thine Own Have We Given Thee: A Liturgical Theology of the Offertory in Anglicanism.*" Eugene, OR: Pickwick Publications, 2023.

Taft, Robert. *Beyond East and West: Problems in Liturgical Understanding.* Washington, D.C.: The Pastoral Press, 1984.

———. "Liturgy as Theology." *Worship* 56, no. 2 (March 1982): 113-117.

———. "Structural Analysis of Liturgical Units: An Essay in Methodology." *Worship* 52, no. 4 (July 1978): 314–29.

Tanner, Kathryn. "In Praise of Open Communion: A Rejoinder to James Farwell." *Anglican Theological Review* 86, no. 3 (Sum 2004): 473-485.

Tanner, Mary. "Anglican." In *The Oxford Handbook of Ecumenical Studies*, 84-100. Edited by Geoffrey Wainwright and Paul McPartlan. Oxford: Oxford University Press, 2021.

Tertullian. "Treatise on Baptism." Translated by S. Thelwall. In *Baptism: Ancient Liturgies and Patristic Texts* by André Hamman, 30-47. New York: Alba House, 1967.

Theissen, Gerd. *The Gospels in Context: Social and Political History in the Synoptic Tradition*. Tranlated by Linda M. Maloney. Minneapolis: Fortress Press, 1991.

Theology Committee of the House of Bishops of the Episcopal Church, "Reflection on Holy Baptism and the Holy Eucharist," *Anglican Theological Review* 93 (Winter 2011): 143-151.

Thurian, Max, ed. *Churches respond to BEM*, Vol. I. Geneva: World Council of Churches, 1986.

_____. *Churches respond to BEM*, Vol. II. Geneva: World Council of Churches, 1986.

_____. *Churches respond to BEM*, Vol. III. Geneva: World Council of Churches, 1987.

_____. *Churches respond to BEM*, Vol. VI. Geneva: World Council of Churches, 1988.

"The Virginia Report." Anglican Consultative Council, 1997. Accessed May 2, 2024, at http://www.lambethconference.org/1998/documents/report-1.pdf.

Wainwright, Geoffrey. *Doxology*. New York: Oxford University Press, 1980.

Ward, W. Reginald and Heitzenrater, Richard P., eds. *The Works of John Wesley*, vol. 19. Nashville, TN: Abingdon Press, 1990.

Ware, Kallistos and Davey, Colin, eds. *Anglican-Orthodox Dialogue*. London: SPCK, 1977.

Weil, Louis. "Baptismal Ecclesiology: Uncovering a Paradigm." In *Equipping the Saints: Ordination in Anglicanism Today*, edited by Ronald L. Dowling and David R. Holeton, 18-34. Dublin: The Columbia Press, 2006.

Welker, Michael. *What Happens in Holy Communion?* Grand Rapids: Eerdmans, 2000.

Westerfield Tucker, Karen. "Baptism and Ecumenism: Agreements and Problems on the Journey toward Mutual Recognition." Presidential address at the Societas Liturgica meeting, August 8-13, 2011.

Winkler, Gabriele. "Confirmation or Chrismation: A Study in Comparative Liturgy." *Worship* 58, no. 1 (January 1984): 2-17.

Zizioulas, John. *Being as Communion*. Crestwood, NY: St. Vladimir's Seminary Press, 1985.

_____. *Eucharist, Bishop, Church: The Unity of the Church in the Divine Eucharist and the Bishop during the First Three Centuries*. Brookline, MA: Holy Cross Orthodox Press, 2001.

_____. "Ordination—A Sacrament? An Orthodox Reply." In *The Plurality of Ministries*. Edited by Hans Kung and Walter Kasper. New York: Herder and Herder, 1972.

INDEX

A

Afanasiev, Nicholas, 112-114, 118-121, 124, 135, 155
Apostolic
    Church, 10, 13, 17, 113, 153
    Succession, 60, 116-117, 156
Apostolic Tradition, 34, 38
Augustine of Hippo, 39-41, 43, 45, 71, 104, 110, 144
Avis, Paul, 109-112, 116-117, 127, 129, 137, 143-147, 155, 175-179

B

Baptism, Eucharist, and Ministry (BEM), ix, 151-154, 156-161, 168-171
Barth, Karl, xvii-xviii, 143
Bobertz, Charles, 14-16, 18
Bradshaw, Paul F., 9, 17, 30, 32, 34-35, 65

C

Chrysostom, John, 41-42, 146
Chupungco, Anscar, 70-71
Cochrane, Arthur, xiv-xvi
Communion
    Before Baptism, xi, xiii, 10, 106
    Without Baptism, xi-xviii, 1-2, 7-9, 13, 19, 27, 84, 96, 98-101, 105-106, 134, 140, 151-153, 164, 167-173, 176-179, 183
Confirmation Rubric, 51-52, 56
Creeds
    Apostles, 6, 82
    Nicene, 6, 51
Cyprian, 33-34, 40, 45, 71, 143

D

Didache, 9-10, 13, 17-18
Dix, Gregory, 35, 39, 65

E

Ecclesiology
    Anglican, 110
    Baptismal, 109, 121-124, 126-133, 141, 154, 157
    Baptismal-eucharistic, xii, 107, 109, 132-143, 145-147, 149, 151, 157-160, 162-166, 168, 181, 185
    Episcopal Succession, 109, 116, 120, 137, 142, 156, 162
    Eucharistic, 109, 118-122, 124-125, 128, 130-131, 133, 135, 142, 155, 157
    Eucharistic baptismal, 133
    National or universal, 109, 111-112, 114-115, 142
Ecumenical Movement, 56, 58, 143, 145, 149, 152, 154, 162, 169, 173-176, 179, 181

Edmonson, Stephen, xvi, 1, 8, 84, 96-100, 105-106, 133
Episkopé, 156-157
Erickson, John H., 121, 128, 131
Evangelical Lutheran Church in America (ELCA), 162-163
Exorcism, 36, 41-42, 47, 50, 52-53, 58-59, 72, 92, 101, 106

F

Fabian, Richard, xv-xvi, 1
Fagerburg, David, 75, 102-103
Ferguson, Everett, 3, 6

G

Gibson, Paul, 130, 132-133

H

Hatchett, Marion, 79, 85, 88-89
Hermeneutical/Hermeneutics, 2, 12-13, 20, 27
    Canonical Criticism, 25-27
    Form Criticism, 22-23
        Sitz im Leben, 6, 22-24, 26
    Grammatical-historical, 21
    Historical-critical, 20-21, 24-25

I

Inculturation, 70-71
Irwin, Kevin, 102

J

Johnson, Maxwell E., 6-7, 33-41, 43, 47

Juxtaposition(s), 5, 76, 91-92, 95-96, 107

K

Kavanaugh, Aidan, 75, 104, 123
Kaye, Bruce, 123, 126-127
Kilmartin, Edward J., 5, 9, 45-47

L

Larson-Miller, Lizette, 130-131
Lathrop, Gordon, vii, 11-15, 18, 76, 91-93, 102
LaVerdiere, Eugene, 4, 8-9
Liturgical Movement, 56, 58, 72, 92

M

Marcus, Joel, 13-14
Martyr, Justin, 30
Meyers, Ruth A., 57-60, 63, 122-123
Miles, Sara, xvi
Minear, Paul, 143
Mitchell, Leonel, 105

N

Narratives
    Feeding, xiv, 9, 11, 13-14, 19
    Infancy, 23, 26
    Syrophoenician Woman, 10-11, 13-15, 18-19

O

Ordo, xv, xvii-xviii, 1-2, 26, 75-78, 80, 82, 87-89, 91, 95-97, 99, 101,

105-107, 125, 136, 153, 166, 173, 178-179, 182, 184
Orthodox/Orthodoxy, xii, 56, 57, 104, 119, 121, 125, 128-129, 132, 155, 159, 163

P

Pauline Theology, 13, 16
Prayer Book Studies (PBS), 59, 61-63, 72
Presbyterian Church (U.S.A.), 159-160, 165-166

Q

Quam Primum, 43-44, 49-50, 69, 72, 106

R

Ridley, Nicholas, 48
Rite(s)
    Communion, 51, 68
    Entrance, 68
    Hand-laying, 35, 38-39, 42-44, 69, 97
    Initiatory/Initiation, 39, 43-45, 47, 49, 55, 59-61, 63-64, 72-73, 75, 78, 86, 92, 96-97, 101, 106, 133, 158
    Latin Sarum, 48
    Liturgical, 34, 44, 62, 64-65, 68-71, 75, 101
    Private, 47-50
    Public, 47, 49-50
    Purification/Purity, xv, xviii, 7, 15-16, 19, 101, 106, 179
    Roman, 43-44
    Unified Initiatory, 59, 61, 64, 72
Roman Catholic, xii, 56-57, 104, 111-112 117, 119, 144, 152, 158, 164

S

Schmemann, Alexander, 75-77, 91, 102
Seabury, Samuel, 54-55
Stamm, Mark, xiv-1, 7-8, 172-173, 178
Standing Liturgical Commission (SLC), 58-60, 62-63

T

Taft, Robert, 66-69, 75-76, 91, 102
Tanner, Kathryn, xvi-xvii, 1, 8, 152, 174
Tertullian, 32-33, 144
Theologia Prima, 75-76, 102-103, 105
Theologia Secunda, 76, 103
Theology
    Baptismal, 16, 18, 40-42, 50, 53, 59, 83, 85
    Eucharistic, 45, 54, 168
    Liturgical, 75-77, 80, 90-91, 96-99, 102-106, 134, 178
    Of the Cross (*Theologica Crucis*), 14
Transubstantiation, 46, 48, 55, 105

U

United Methodist Church (UMC), 160, 169-171, 175

W

Wainwright, Geoffrey, 103-104
Weil, Louis, 126, 132
Wesley, John, 169-172

Westerfield-Tucker, Karen, 171-172
World Council of Churches (WCC), ix, 56-57, 151-153, 157, 167-168

Z

Zizioulas, John, 119-122, 124-125, 128, 132